Sentiment in the Forex Market

Indicators and Strategies to Profit from Crowd Behavior and Market Extremes

JAMIE SAETTELE

WILEY

John Wiley & Sons, Inc.

Published by John Wiley & Sons, Inc., Hoboken, New Jersey.
Published simultaneously in Canada.

For general information on our other products and services or for technical support, please contact our Customer Care Department within the United States at (800) 762-2974, outside the United States at (317) 572-3993 or fax (317) 572-4002.

Wiley also publishes its books in a variety of electronic formats. Some content that appears in print may not be available in electronic books. For more information about Wiley products, visit our web site at www.wiley.com.

Library of Congress Cataloging-in-Publication Data

Saettele, Jamie, 1982–
    Sentiment in the forex market : indicators and strategies to profit from crowd behavior and market extremes / Jamie Saettele.
        p.   cm.—(Wiley trading series)
    Includes bibliographical references and index.
    ISBN 978-0-470-20823-6 (cloth)
1. Foreign exchange market.   2. Foreign exchange futures.   3. Investment analysis.   I. Title.
    HG3851.S23 2008
    332.4'5—dc22

                                                            2008006112

Printed in the United States of America.

10 9 8 7 6 5 4 3 2 1

To my parents, whose Love inspires me.

Contents

Preface

As public interest in the FX market has skyrocketed, so too has the amount of technical and fundamental research available to aspiring traders. An area that has failed to receive the same amount of attention is often considered part of the technical approach: sentiment. After the news releases are digested by floor traders, the fundamentals digested by economists, and the latest comments from the central banker are dissected, the market's trend is still a product of underlying sentiment. That is the premise of this book. Much (if not most) of the information fed to retail traders is of little use when it comes to making money by trading. Trading is hardly as simple as buying or selling, because an economic indicator is good or bad. Similarly, the game is not as black or white as buying or selling, because price is above or below a moving average.

For one, I hope to prove that traditional approaches such as the economic indicator approach do not work. No consistent correlation exists between the U.S. dollar and U.S. economic indicators, but conventional wisdom says that the two move in lockstep. Why is this approach followed so fervently if its foundation is rooted in falsities? The reason that markets move in identifiable patterns is probably the same reason that many accept as gospel the conventional approaches to market analysis and trading that have marginally successful track records at best. That reason is the propensity for humans to follow the crowd, especially in situations as emotionally driven as trading. Although there are no doubt very successful news traders, the cost to the trader is significant: an expensive machine such as Bloomberg or Reuters, turbulent market conditions just after a news release, and most important—the emotional impulses that are our worst enemy in trading are heightened, and the ability to make a rational decision just after a news release is greatly reduced. I think that I can share with you a better (and cheaper) approach to analyzing and trading the FX market, an approach that will give you an edge, if only because you are not following the crowd.

Sentiment indicators such as the Commitments of Traders reports are followed by many market participants, but I have developed indicators with the data that are meant to pinpoint the few times each year that a market is likely to reverse. This helps to solve one of the biggest obstacles that many face: over-trading. By limiting yourself to making a decision when a specific set of circumstances are met, you are helping to solve the over-trading problem. Unconventional sentiment indicators such as news headlines and magazine covers offer some of the best trading signals every year. Not to be forgotten are more traditional technical tools such as RSI and slow stochastics. Is the conventional use, to indicate overbought and oversold levels, really the best way to go? I think that there is a better way.

What you will not find in this book are trade setups with rigid rules or money management tips. Markets are dynamic and the trader should be also. Money management will be different for everyone because everyone has an entirely different risk tolerance. What I hope that this book provides is a way for you to look at a specific market (and maybe others) for what it truly is: a collection of its participants that create a mind of its own, whose moves are endogenous in nature but, because of that very reason, can be exploited for profit.

Acknowledgments

I want to thank everyone that I work with at DailyFX but in particular Kathy Lien, who gave me a chance at DailyFX and convinced me to pursue this endeavor, Antonio Sousa, whose help with program trading through the years is indispensable, and Boris Schlossberg. Although Boris and I disagree on almost everything market related, he has helped me realize that more perspectives lead to a better perspective.

CHAPTER 1

The Argument
for a
Sentiment-Based
Approach

A t its core, sentiment is a general thought, feeling, or sense. In free markets, sentiment refers to the feelings and emotions of market participants. All of the participants' feelings toward a specific market result in a dominant psychology that is either optimistic or pessimistic. Every change in price results from a change in the balance between optimism and pessimism. Price itself is a result of where collective psychology lies in the never-ending oscillation between optimism and pessimism. As oscillation suggests, the psychological state of a market experiences peaks (optimistic extreme) and troughs (pessimistic extreme). These sentiment extremes are what affect market tops and bottoms.

In the 1932 edition of Charles Mackay's classic *Extraordinary Popular Delusions and the Madness of Crowds*, Bernard Baruch wrote in the foreword that "all economic movements, by their very nature, are motivated by crowd psychology." Baruch went on to write in the same foreword that "without due recognition of crowd-thinking (which often seems crowd-madness) our theories of economics leave much to be desired."[1] It seems that so many, if not most, of the members of the financial community seem to forget these basic truths. Analysts, traders, and financial media members attribute reasons to price movements with an uncanny ease.

For example, "The government reported a larger than expected increase in the number of jobs created, which supported the U.S. dollar." Forget that the same report one month earlier indicated that fewer jobs were created than expected...and the dollar rallied anyway. On that day, the headline probably read something like this: Dollar Rallies Despite Downbeat Jobs Report. These examples are hypothetical, but if you follow the currency market, you have undoubtedly witnessed similar inconsistencies in financial reporting. How can the movement of a currency be attributed to an outside event such as the release of an economic indicator one month when the same currency and same economic indicator show absolutely no relationship in other months? If a relationship exists only some of the time, then by definition there is no consistent relationship. Yet, the majority of market participants base trading decisions on economic indicators anyway. Why? Even though the approach is suspect, it is conventional and popular and humans like to be with the crowd, even if they are wrong. It is much easier to be wrong in a crowd than be wrong by yourself.

Baruch also wrote in the foreword of *Extraordinary Popular Delusions and the Madness of Crowds* that:

> *Entomologists may be able to answer the question about the midges and to say what force creates such unitary movement by thousands of individuals, but I have never seen the answer. The migration of some types of birds; the incredible mass performance of the whole species of ocean eels; the prehistoric tribal human eruptions from Central Asia; the Crusades; the mediaeval dance crazes; or, getting closer to economics, the Mississippi and South Sea Bubbles; the Tulip Craze; and (are we too close to add?) the Florida boom and the 1929 market-madness in America and its sequences in 1930 and 1931—all these are phenomena of mass action under impulsions and controls which no science has explored. They have power unexpectedly to affect any static condition or so-called normal trend. For that reason, they have place in the considerations of thoughtful students of world economic conditions.*[2]

The last example that Baruch cited, the 1929 stock market crash, may be on the verge of repeating as I write this book in late 2007. The herding instinct is a fact of human nature and manifests itself in all our speculative activities; whether real estate, stock markets, or currency valuations. Markets move in trends but reverse at extreme levels of bullishness (tops) and bearishness (bottoms) as English economist Arthur C. Pigou explained: "An error of optimism tends to create a certain measure of psychological interdependence until it leads to a crisis. Then the error of optimism dies and gives birth to an error of pessimism."[3]

This is the rule in all financial markets, where man's impulse to herd creates extreme and unsustainable levels that ultimately lead to a reversal. Markets always overshoot and do not seek equilibrium as the Efficient Market Hypothesis (EMH) would have you believe.

A popular (if not the most popular) model used to trade foreign exchange (FX) among retail traders is based on economic indicators. Under this approach, a trader will buy a country's currency if the news of that country is considered good. If the news of a country's currency is considered bad, then the trader sells that country's currency. This model assumes that EMH governs markets because it assumes that market participants will make objective trading decisions based on rational thought (buy if the news is good and sell if the news is bad). However, market participants do not make objective trading decisions based on rational thought; they make subjective trading decisions based on emotions. If you have ever traded FX, then you know this because you have witnessed a currency rally that followed a worse than expected jobs report or an increase in that country's trade deficit. Still, the news was explained in order to rationalize the market movement. If explaining the news in order to rationalize the market movement proves too difficult, then the market move is often attributed to a "technical" correction or something similar.

This is not to say that news and economic releases are unimportant. It is imperative that you know *when* the releases occur because volatility spikes during these times as a great number of traders are involved in the market. Sometimes the correct move is to fade the initial reaction. For example, you are a sentiment-based trader and your analysis indicates that sentiment is turning from a euro bullish extreme. After a supposedly bullish euro new release, the EURUSD spikes 50 pips, right into a resistance area. Your bigger picture analysis suggests that the best move is to sell this rally. Sure enough, the EURUSD retraces all of its post news release gains within a few hours.

How do we know for certain that herding occurs in financial markets and particularly in FX? This book is dedicated to proving that it does occur in FX and to showing how you can take advantage of it. If markets were truly governed by the EMH model, which is the foundation for more conventional approaches to trading FX (such as the economic indicator model), then why do most news headlines and stories about a currency appear when that currency is at an important top or bottom? Why are those headlines increasingly optimistic as price rises and increasingly pessimistic as price declines? Why do more speculators buy as price increases and sell as price decreases? This last reality runs contrary to traditional economic supply and demand models that demand decreases as price increases. The only explanation for such behavior is that speculators are not thinking rationally when they make trading decisions. If they did, then a greater number of traders would buy low and sell high. What really happens though is that most buy high and sell low. The result is that most traders (probably 90 to 95 percent in FX) lose money and only a select few make a lot of money. If you understand this concept, then you can exploit it and be one of the few that does make money.

WHAT IS FUNDAMENTAL?

Anyone who is any good at anything will tell you that preparation is just as important, if not more important, than whatever it is that you are preparing for. Successful actors research their roles before filming begins. Sports teams practice and watch films of their opponents before they play against them. Similarly, in order to trade successfully (especially in a highly leveraged market such as FX), you must have a plan, an approach. An approach should not consist of buying because an economic indicator was strong or selling because the same economic indicator was weak. You probably have gathered by now that I do not find value in traditional fundamentals. What is considered "fundamental"—primarily economic indicators—is not actually fundamental to price at all. The charts in Chapter 2 support this claim.

Although I lean toward a technician's point of view, a successful approach to market analysis and trading is not as simple as buying because price is above the moving average or selling because price is below the moving average. Trading is hardly this black and white. A grasp of what is really fundamental to a market's movement—sentiment—is the key to success in the game of trading and speculation.

TOP-DOWN APPROACH

The trader must process information (preparation) before making a decision (the trade). There are two approaches to processing information: *top-down* and *bottom-up*. When implementing a top-down approach, information regarding the big picture is gathered first.

Big picture is the sentiment backdrop as defined by analysis of indicators such as (but not limited to) the U.S. Commodity Futures Trading Commission's (CFTC's) Commitment of Traders (COT) reports. Does futures positioning indicate that the currency in question is at or is nearing an optimistic or pessimistic extreme? Is the financial media providing any signals? It may sound unconventional (because it is—which is probably why it works), but the financial media often provides exceptionally timely signals. It is just as important to know when a market is not extreme because sometimes the best thing to do is nothing; sit with the trade you have on and ride the trend. There is a time to be a contrarian, but it is less often than most think. Some traders are contrarians just to be contrarians; they are always fighting the trend and never make money.

After you feel that you have correctly gauged the psychological state of the market, it is time to assess your risk and time your trade. Knowledge of the market's structure is essential to this next step. All markets exhibit the same patterns, on all time frames. This is known as the Elliott wave principle, or simply the wave principle. In the 1930s, Ralph Nelson Elliott discovered that crowd behavior will trend and countertrend in recognizable patterns. Although he primarily studied the stock market, the wave principle can be applied to any freely traded market. The size of the FX market makes it a perfect candidate for an analysis technique based on crowd behavior. You will be amazed at the accuracy with which you can gauge support and resistance and forecast direction and the extent of the directional move with knowledge of the wave principle.

Traditional technical indicators such as moving averages and oscillators aid in identifying the trend but should be used as secondary tools to sentiment indicators and price patterns. After all, you are trading price, not the indicator.

The goal of this book is to provide the tools necessary for developing a top-down, sentiment-based approach to trading and speculation in FX. I refrain from providing specifics such as entries or risk control because these are aspects of trading that everyone will approach differently.

REMINISCENCES OF A STOCK OPERATOR

If there is one trading book that has had a profound impact on me, then without a doubt that book is *Reminiscences of a Stock Operator*, written in 1923 by Edwin Lefévre. The fictionalized biography of Jesse Livermore (some say that he actually wrote it), one of Wall Street's all-time great speculators, the story is told through the eyes of the fictional Larry Livingston. (Livermore was the inspiration for Livingston.) Livingston's experiences and related commentary ring true to the point that it is hard to believe that Livermore himself did not write the book. Regardless of who wrote it, the book is responsible for many of the trading adages that are so common throughout the trading community. When I hit a trading rut, because of bad habits or simply flawed thinking, I always go back to *Reminiscences* for a reread and it always helps. If you have yet to do so, I strongly recommend reading *Reminiscences*.

I have compiled a few quotes from the book that I believe capture the importance of sentiment in trading and speculation.[4]

Market Dynamics Are Timeless

"Another lesson I learned early is that there is nothing new in Wall Street. There can't be because speculation is as old as the hills. Whatever happens . . . has happened before and will happen again."

"Nowhere does history indulge in repetitions so often or so uniformly as in Wall Street. When you read contemporary accounts of booms or panics the one thing that strikes you most forcibly is how little either speculators or speculation today differ from yesterday. The game does not change and neither does human nature."

Translation: Sentiment has been, is, and always will be fundamental to price in any market. Price patterns that occurred 50 or 100 years ago occur now and will occur in the future. A market price is determined by fear and greed, which is manifested through the activities of the market participants; traders, investors, speculators, and the like. This will never change.

Human Nature

"But in actual practice a man has to guard against many things, and most of all against himself—that is, against human nature."

"I sometimes think that speculation must be an unnatural sort of business, because I find that the average speculator has arrayed against him his own nature. The weaknesses that all men are prone to are fatal to success in speculation—usually those very weaknesses that make him likable to his fellows or that he himself particularly guards against in those other ventures of his where there are not nearly so dangerous as when he is trading in stocks or commodities."

"The speculator's chief enemies are always boring from within. It is inseparable from human nature to hope and to fear. In speculation when the market goes against you hope that every day will be the last day—and you lose more than you should had you not listened to hope—to the same ally that is so potent a success—bringer to empire builders, big and little. And when the market goes your way you become fearful that the next day will take away your profit, and you get out—too soon. Fear keeps you from making as much money as you ought to. The successful trader has to fight these two deep-seated instincts. He has to reverse what you might call his natural impulses. Instead of hoping he must fear; instead of fearing he must hope. He must fear that his loss may develop into a much bigger loss. And hope that his profit may become a big profit."

"I have come to feel that it is as necessary to know how to read myself as to know how to read the tape."

"On the other hand there is profit in studying the human factors—the ease with which human beings believe what it pleases them to believe; and how they allow themselves—indeed, urge themselves—to be influenced by their cupidity or by the dollar-cost average man's carelessness. Fear and hope remain the same; therefore the study of the psychology of speculators is as valuable as it ever was."

"The principles of successful stock speculation are based on the supposition that people will continue in the future to make the mistakes that they have made in the past."

"The speculators' deadly enemies are: Ignorance, greed, fear, and hope. All the statute books in the world and all the rules of all the exchanges on earth cannot eliminate these from the human animal."

Translation: It is natural for humans to follow the crowd. Following the crowd is ingrained in our DNA and is a big reason why our species has succeeded to the extent that we have. Following the crowd, in a general sense, has helped us thrive as far back as when we were hunter-gatherers. We feel safer as part of a crowd. It is easier to be wrong as part of a crowd. However, in the end, the crowd is wrong in matters of financial speculation.

A trader's main competition is not other traders, but him- or herself. Most traders lose money because our emotional impulses act as a barrier to successful speculation. The only way to overcome this barrier is to be cognizant of it.

I am not sure that it is possible to better explain the role that the human factor plays in markets than with the above quotations. Not everyone agrees, which is fine. This is one view, but I believe it is correct. There are many out there who have enjoyed success approaching the game another way. You must decide which approach works for you.

The rest of this book presents a framework that you can use to gauge where the market of your choice is in the never-ending oscillation between optimism and pessimism; so that you can trade accordingly.

CHAPTER 2

The Problem with Fundamental Analysis

T wo forms dominate analysis and trading: fundamental and technical. The two methods of analysis have led to a philosophical divide among analysts, traders, and the entire financial community. I have problems with both methods in the traditional sense, but especially "fundamental" analysis. The traditional fundamental approach is backward looking, which is great for attempting to explain why something did happen but worthless if attempting to forecast what could happen.

In the FX market, fundamental analysis refers to analysis of a country's economic conditions. This includes macroeconomic indicators such as growth rates, interest rates and monetary policy, inflation, and unemployment. The fundamental analyst and/or trader believes that he or she can analyze these macroeconomic indicators, arrive at a bullish or bearish bias regarding the currency in question, and trade accordingly. *Reminiscences of a Stock Operator* sums up the effectiveness of trading based strictly on news events (economic indicators are considered news events). The main character, Larry Livingston, remarks that "the trend has been established before the news is published, and in all bull markets bear items are ignored and bull news items exaggerated; and vice versa."[1] This was true in 1923 when *Reminiscences* was first published, and it is true today.

Most new traders believe that economic indicators somehow possess the secret to a successful trading strategy and do not even think about questioning this conventional approach. When entering a new endeavor, it is human nature to take the conventional approach, in other words, to follow the crowd. Following the crowd is deeply ingrained in our brains and for good reason. The herd mentality is essential to survival. Something as general as "fitting in," whether child or adult (usually learned in childhood), is a general example of following the crowd. This includes talking, acting, or dressing in a certain way in order to be accepted and become part of society. One could argue, however, that criminals fail to follow the crowd in some respects and as a result fail to become part of society. It could be argued that the rejection of conventional approaches such as going to school, getting a job, and so forth, results in neglect from society, which leads to criminal life. Most would agree that following the crowd as it is presented in these examples is paramount to success in life.

The opposite is true when considering financial speculation (currency trading, in this case). The conventional approach (the approach that the crowd follows), which relies on studying economic indicators in order to trade the FX market, does not work in my opinion. One look at a chart disproves the myth that a positive correlation exists between economic indicators and currency values over any meaningful time period.

More than 90 percent of all currency trades involve the U.S. dollar; therefore, consistent correlations should exist between the greenback and various U.S. economic indicators. This hypothesis seems rational so it must be true. Therein lies the problem with this thinking. In freely traded markets, decisions are based not on rational thought but on emotions. In order to understand why emotions rule markets, it is necessary to take a look at the construction of the human brain.

HOW THE HUMAN BRAIN WORKS

In *The Wave Principle of Human Social Behavior*, Robert Prechter cites the research of Paul MacLean, former head of the Laboratory for Brain Evolution at the National Institute of Mental Health, in order to explain from a biological perspective why investment and trading decisions are based on emotions, not rational thought. In *The Triune Brain in Evolution*, MacLean proposes that the brain consists of three parts: the R-complex, the limbic system, and the neocortex. The R-complex is the part of the brain that humans share with other animals and even reptiles. The reptilian brain includes the brain stem and cerebellum, which controls survival instincts such as muscles, balance, breathing, and heartbeat. The limbic system is found only in mammals and controls emotions and instincts such as feeding, fighting, sexual behavior, and herding. The neocortex is found in higher mammals and is significantly developed in humans. This portion of the brain controls reason and speech. In summary, the human brain consists of three distinct parts: primal, emotional, and rational.[2]

Scientific research has found that the limbic system, the emotional part of the brain, works faster than the neocortex. This describes why "feelings of certainty can be so overwhelming that they stand fast in the face of logic and contradiction. They can attach themselves to a political doctrine, a social plan, the verity of religion, the surety of winning on the next spin of the roulette wheel, the presumed path of a financial market or any other idea."[3] In other words, emotion trumps rational thought. Financial speculation induces herding behavior, which is controlled by the limbic system. "As a primitive tool of survival, emotional impulses from the limbic system impel a desire among individuals to seek signals from others in matters of knowledge and behavior and therefore to align their feelings and convictions with those of the group."[4] Most market participants' ideas stem from other market participants, which leads to the creation of a crowd. "They are driven to follow the herd because they do not have firsthand knowledge adequate to form an independent conviction, which makes them seek wisdom in numbers. The unconscious says, You have too little basis upon which to exercise reason; your only alternative is to assume that the herd knows where it's going."[5] The sentiment indicators that we will examine later prove that market participants herd. By definition, *herding* means that the emotional part of the brain, the limbic system, is in charge. Remember, this is the same part of the brain that controls fighting and the emotion of love. Do you ever think rationally when it comes to fighting or love? Similarly, the neocortex (rational thought) is subservient in financial speculation. Therefore, the study of sentiment indicators, or the study of crowds, is more important than the study of economic indicators, if you wish to make money trading.

The charts in this chapter support this assertion. What most assume is important regarding currency valuation actually has little impact, aside from knee-jerk reactions just after the economic release.

THE MYTH OF ECONOMIC INDICATORS

As mentioned earlier, one would think that since more than 90 percent of all currency trades involve the U.S. dollar, consistent correlations would exist between the dollar and various economic indicators. But we know that the emotional part of the brain rules decision making during financial speculation, which is a herding process, so it is unlikely that there is a consistent correlation. If there were consistent correlations between the U.S. dollar and economic indicators, then one would have to assume that trading decisions were being based on rational thought, which simply is not the case.

All of the charts shown here are monthly (since the indicators that we are looking at are released once a month) and the correlations are 3-year (36-month) correlations. The economic indicators that are assumed to be of utmost importance when it comes to valuation of the U.S. dollar are the nonfarm payrolls report (Employment Situation), the Treasury International Capital number (investment flows), the U.S. trade balance, gross domestic product, and the Consumer and Producer Price indexes. I have included rather detailed descriptions of the economic indicators as well. If you are going to enter into a debate with someone who contends that economic indicators are the secret to trading success, then it is wise to know what you are arguing about. You will also see that some of the ways in which the economic numbers are calculated are suspect, to say the least.

NONFARM PAYROLLS

On the first Friday of the month, the Employment Situation report is released by the Bureau of Labor Statistics (BLS). To be honest, the release of the indicator can, and often does, lead to one of the more exciting days to be in the market. It makes sense that analysts and traders would assume that employment is critical to currency valuation. A country that cannot employ its citizens is certainly facing economic problems. In the United States, consumer spending accounts for roughly 70 percent of gross domestic product (GDP). A loss of jobs will most likely lead to a decrease in discretionary income, which leads to a decline in consumer spending, which leads to a decline in GDP (we will look at GDP later). It seems logical that the release of the Employment Situation report would be a main determinant in the price of the Dollar Index (DXY), and by extension the EURUSD, GBPUSD, USDJPY, and so forth. However, remember that the market is far from logical. Believing that the market will move based on what should be logical is the kind of thinking that gets us in trouble in trading.

The big number within the Employment Situation, and the number that we will examine, is the change in nonfarm payrolls. The calculation of the employment statistics includes people age 16 and older. The BLS defines employed people as those who have worked and been paid for their work by someone else or by themselves. Those who are on leave from a job, paid or unpaid, are also considered employed. Examples include maternity or paternity leave, illness, or vacation. Unemployed people are those who have either quit or been fired. There are several types of unemployment. Richard Yamarone defines the various types of unemployment in *The Trader's Guide to Key Economic Indicators*:

> *Seasonal unemployment results from short-term cyclical changes in the labor market; examples include the January layoffs of retail staff who were added to take care of the Christmas shopping push, and the winter furloughs of construction and landscaping workers in regions where harsh weather makes such activity virtually impossible. Frictional unemployment refers to the situation of workers in the process of changing occupations who are temporarily between jobs. Structural unemployment is the result of economic restructuring caused by new technologies or other innovations, as when the invention of the automobile put buggy-whip makers out of a job. Finally, cyclical unemployment occurs when jobs are eliminated as part of the business cycle, because of declining demand and the consequent drop in production.*[6]

Interestingly, in order to be considered unemployed, a person must be actively seeking work. The homeless guy in the alley and others who are not looking for a job are not counted in the labor force. As a result, a low unemployment rate can be misleading. If a large number of people stop looking for work, then the number of people in the labor force declines. If the number of people employed remains the same, then the unemployment rate declines as a result and suggests that the employment situation is better than it really is. For this reason, fundamental analysts tend to prefer to look at the change in nonfarm payrolls, which details the number of jobs created.

With all of this employment information fresh in your mind, it is time to take a look at a chart of DXY and the monthly change in nonfarm payrolls. As mentioned, the indicator is released once a month; therefore, the chart in Figure 2.1 is a monthly chart. The DXY is on the top, the monthly change in nonfarm payrolls is below the DXY, and the three-year correlation between the two is on the bottom.

What Does the Chart Say?

Just looking at the correlation, it is obvious that there are extended periods of time when the DXY and the change in nonfarm payrolls are correlated and uncorrelated. A negative correlation can be seen from June 1974 to May 1979, September 1982 to November 1983, April 1987 to March 1990, and November 1997 to June 2006. A positive correlation exists from August 1979 to June 1982, January 1984 to February 1987, June 1990 to

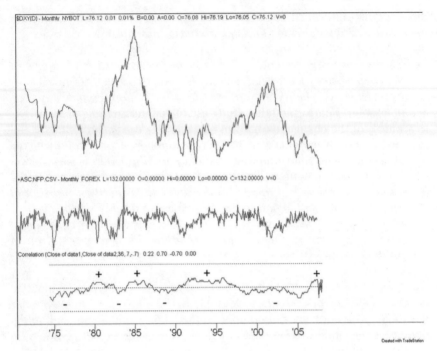

FIGURE 2.1 A 36-month (3-year) correlation of the DXY and change in NFP show that no consistent correlation exists
Source: Chart created on TradeStation®, the flagship product of TradeStation Technologies, Inc.

March 1997, and August 2006 to present (July 2007). In all, there was a negative correlation for 215 months and a positive correlation for 158 months. Based on these figures, one cannot say that the change in nonfarm payrolls affects the DXY. There is no consistent correlation.

The relationship (or lack of) between the DXY and the change in nonfarm payrolls can be viewed in a different manner. Does the DXY tend to peak when the change in nonfarm payrolls peaks? If so, then a trader could use this information to gauge tops and bottoms in the DXY by turning bearish when the change in nonfarm payrolls is peaking and turning bullish when the change in nonfarm payrolls is bottoming. The major tops in the DXY occurred in January 1974, June 1976, February 1985, June 1989, July 1991, February 1994, July 2001, and November 2005. None of these months match with peaks (± 3 months) in the change in nonfarm payrolls. Interestingly, one of the peaks in the DXY matches up with a bottom in the payrolls change. The July 2001 top in the DXY occurred three months before a bottom was registered for the change in nonfarm payrolls. With knowledge of this data, anyone contending that job creation and the U.S. dollar are positively correlated would have to assume that more jobs are actually bad for the U.S. dollar. Regardless, the chart makes it clear that highs and lows in job creation are not correlated with highs and lows in the DXY.

Many will take issue with this study because I am not taking into account the expected change in nonfarm payrolls and comparing that to the actual number. I performed that study as well. Many analysts assume that the release of the change in nonfarm payrolls sets the trading tone for the rest of the month, especially if the actual number significantly deviates from the consensus. Since the Employment Situation report is released on the first Friday of the month, this is a logical but false assumption. I gathered the average estimate and the actual number for the change in nonfarm payrolls from July 1998 until present (July 2007). This is 110 months of data. I subtracted the average survey (expected number) from the actual number to find out if the change in nonfarm payrolls exceeded or failed to exceed market expectations. A positive number indicates that the number exceeded expectations, and a negative number indicates that the number failed to meet expectations. The standard deviation of the difference is 92,000 (rounded). In statistics, a difference of two standard deviations or more is considered a significant difference. In other words, if the difference between the estimate and the actual number is at least 184,000 (92,000 × 2), then the difference is considered extreme. If a significant positive difference consistently shows up with a monthly *gain* in the DXY and if a significant negative difference consistently shows up with a monthly *loss* in the DXY, then it makes sense to assume that when the actual change in nonfarm payrolls significantly deviates from the consensus estimate, the trading tone is set for the rest of the month in the direction of the difference. If there is no consistent correlation, then the assumption is incorrect. The results are displayed in Table 2.1.

Significant differences (more than two standard deviations, which we found to be 184,000) occurred in July 1999, November 1999, August 2000,

TABLE 2.1 Significant Differences in Actual vs. Expected NFP Change

Month	Actual-Expected NFP	USD Index % Change	Result
July 1999	−206	−3.01	Agree
November 1999	−227	2.99	Disagree
August 1999	−251	2.77	Disagree
June 2001	−237	0.36	Disagree
April 2003	−312	−1.91	Agree
May 2004	188	−1.91	Disagree
September 2004	−206	−1.74	Agree

June 2001, April 2003, May 2004, and September 2004. The only positive difference, where the jobs created were far more than expected, was May 2004. Interestingly, May 2004 was a positive surprise of more than 188,000, yet the DXY actually fell 1.91 percent that month. All of the other differences were negative surprises. In other words, the jobs created were far less than expected. The conventional approach assumes that a negative surprise is negative for the dollar so the DXY should fall during those months. The dollar did fall in July 1999 (significant loss), April 2003, and September 2004, but the dollar gained in November 1999 (significant gain), August 2000 (significant gain), and June 2001 (not much of a gain). The evidence indicates that the change in nonfarm payrolls, even changes that deviate significantly from the consensus, has absolutely no effect on the trend of the DXY.

GROSS DOMESTIC PRODUCT

Gross domestic product (GDP) is considered the "broadest, most comprehensive barometer available of a country's overall economic condition. GDP is the sum of the market values of all final goods and services produced in a country during a specific period using that country's resources, regardless of the ownership of the resources."[7] GDP includes data on personal income and consumption expenditures, corporate profits, national income, and inflation. In the United States, GDP is reported quarterly and by the Commerce Department's Bureau of Economic Analysis (BEA). Although released quarterly, there are actually three versions: the advance report, the preliminary report, and the final report. The different versions of the report result in a release every month, but two-thirds of the releases are revisions.

The advance report is released one month following the quarter reported on. The first report of the year then is the advance report for the fourth quarter of the previous year. For example, the advance report for 2006 fourth quarter GDP was released on January 31, 2007. One month later, or two months following the end of the quarter, the preliminary report is released. This is the first revision. The second revision is contained in the final report and is released three months after the end of the quarter. All reports are released at 8:30 A.M. ET. What is interesting is that "annual revisions are calculated during July of every year, based on data that become available to the BEA only on an annual basis . . . The BEA estimates these data on a quarterly basis via a judgmental trend based on annual surveys of state and local governments."[8] In other words, revisions are made every year based on what government officials think. How accurate can these revisions possibly be?

What's more, "every five years the BEA issues a so-called benchmark revision of all of the data. This typically has resulted in considerable changes to the five years of quarterly figures."[9] So five years from now, we will learn that GDP was actually significantly higher or lower than what was originally reported by the BEA. In a sense, the original GDP release is an arbitrary number because it is subject to many different revisions, for up to five years! Basing trading decisions and risking money on this kind of information does not make much sense.

What Does the Chart Say?

Conventional theory and most analysts assume that strong GDP leads to a strong currency. I plotted the annualized GDP growth (final report) on a chart with the DXY to see if there is any correlation (data since 1990). Since GDP is released every quarter and since the largest time frame for the DXY that I have access to is a monthly chart, it was not possible to run an actual correlation (as I did with the DXY and NFP). Still, we can compare the trends of the indicator and the DXY visually in order to determine if there is any correlation. See Figure 2.2.

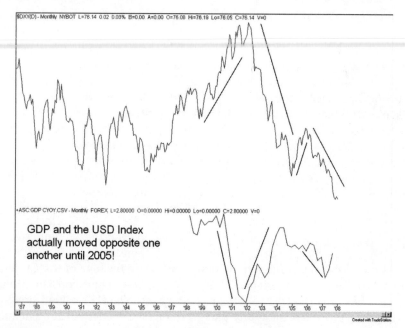

FIGURE 2.2 GDP and the DXY actually moved opposite one another for the better part of the last decade
Source: Chart created on TradeStation®, the flagship product of TradeStation Technologies, Inc.

From March of 1991 to December 1992, GDP growth increased from −1 percent (contracting economy) to 4.1 percent. The DXY actually declined during most of that time, from 96.06 in June 1991 to 78.87 in August 1992. From December 1995 to June 2000, GDP and the DXY exhibited a strong correlation as GDP growth increased from 2 to 4.8 percent and the DXY rallied from 84.76 to 106.84 during the same period. From June 2000 to December 2001 (after the stock market bubble burst in March 2000), GDP growth plummeted from 4.8 to 0.2 percent. However, the DXY continued to rally during the same period, from 106.84 to 120.25. Interestingly, GDP growth rebounded strongly from the December 2001 low of 0.2 to 4.5 percent in June 2004. During that time, the DXY plummeted from 120.25 to 88.80. Since June 2004, the DXY has rallied and declined while GDP growth has mostly declined. Aside from December 1995 to June 2000, when GDP growth and the DXY moved together, the two have actually exhibited a negative correlation.

TRADE BALANCE

A country's trade balance is the value of its net imports subtracted from the value of its net exports over a specific time period. Naturally, the U.S. trade balance is reported, or valued, in U.S. dollars. A country, such as China, that exports more than it imports has a trade surplus. A country that imports more than it exports has a trade deficit. The United States carries the world's largest trade deficit at over $700 billion, or close to $60 billion per month. Many analysts see deficits as detrimental to the currency of the country running the deficit. The thinking is that deficits are corrected by free markets as floating currency rates rise or fall over time in order to encourage exports over imports, reversing again in favor of imports as the currency gains strength. For more information regarding the U.S. trade balance, go to www.bea.gov (Bureau of Economic Analysis).

What Does the Chart Say?

The United States has run a trade deficit (negative balance of trade) since the 1970s. The chart in Figure 2.3 shows that there is no consistent correlation between the DXY and the trade balance. The DXY rallied steadily throughout the 1990s and early part of the next decade to 121.00 in July 2001. During this time, in which the DXY gained 55 percent, the trade deficit multiplied by a factor of nearly 9 (or an increase of 769 percent). Since July 2001, the correlation between the trade balance and the DXY has been a

$DXY(D) - Monthly NYBOT L=76.13 0.02 0.02% B=0.00 A=0.00 O=76.08 Hi=76.19 Lo=76.05 C=76.13 V=0

The trade deficit has steadily increased but the USD Index has rallied and declined significantly during this time.

•ASC:USTB.CSV - Monthly FOREX L=-60.03600 O=0.00000 Hi=0.00000 Lo=0.00000 C=-60.03600 V=0

'84 '85 '86 '87 '88 '89 '90 '91 '92 '93 '94 '95 '96 '97 '98 '99 '00 '01 '02 '03 '04 '05 '06 '07 '08

Created with TradeStation

FIGURE 2.3 Studying the trade balance would get you nowhere if you were trying to forecast the direction of the DXY
Source: Chart created on TradeStation®, the flagship product of TradeStation Technologies, Inc.

positive one. In other words, there is no *consistent* correlation. The DXY could rally and the trade deficit continue to widen, and those who are familiar with this type of chart would not be surprised since that is exactly what has happened before.

TREASURY INTERNATIONAL CAPITAL

The calculations that are done to arrive at the Treasury International Capital (TIC) number are quite complex. Instead of trying to condense everything into a few paragraphs, I have included excerpts from the U.S. Department of the Treasury's web site (www.treas.gov), the entity responsible for data on capital flows in and out of the United States. Understanding the TIC number to this extent is good for general knowledge purposes but will not help in trading. If you're not interested, feel free to skip to Figure 2.4, which

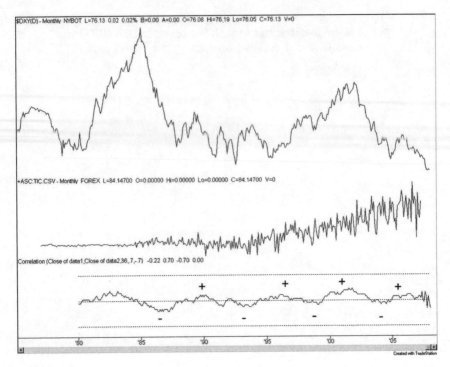

FIGURE 2.4 U.S. Dollar Index Monthly Chart with TIC Data
Source: Chart created on TradeStation®, the flagship product of TradeStation Technologies, Inc.

shows that the TIC number has steadily risen as the DXY has trended up, down, and sideways.

TIC System

The Treasury International Capital (TIC) reporting system is the U.S. government's source of data on capital flows into and out of the United States, excluding direct investment, and the resulting levels of cross-border claims and liabilities. The data is used by the Bureau of Economic Analysis in the computation of the U.S. Balance of Payments accounts and the U.S. International Investment Position. Information is collected from commercial banks and other depository institutions, bank holding companies, securities brokers and dealers, custodians of securities, and nonbanking enterprises in the United States, including the U.S. branches, agencies and subsidiaries of foreign-based banks and business enterprises. The TIC capital movement reports are filed directly with

Federal Reserve Banks, who act as fiscal agents for the Treasury in this function.

Banking Claims and Liabilities

The data series are based on submissions of monthly reports on own dollar liabilities and claims and on certain custody liabilities denominated in dollars. Quarterly reports are filed for liabilities and claims payable in foreign currencies and on dollar claims held for domestic customers. These reports are mandatory and are filed by banks and other depository institutions in the U.S. (including agencies, branches and other banking affiliates of foreign-based banks), International Banking Facilities (IBFs), bank holding companies, and brokers and dealers in the U.S., who, for their own account or for the account of their customers, have reportable liabilities to, or claims on, foreign residents. The data series are revised for up to 24 months after the initial "as of" reporting date. The data are released to the public with a lag of approximately 1 1/2 months. Broadly, these data series include liabilities and claims arising from deposits due to or from foreign entities, financial instruments including short-term negotiable securities such as U.S. Treasury bills and certificates with an original maturity of one year or less, borrowings from foreigners and loans and other credits to foreigners. Banks include their liabilities and claims on foreign branches and other affiliates that arise out of normal banking business; effective February 2003, these data additionally include positions with affiliated foreign offices of brokers and dealers. Excluded from all respondents' reports are direct investments, positions arising from equity securities and debt issues with original maturity of more than one year, contingent items; and off-balance sheet contracts, including unsettled spot and forward foreign exchange contracts, options, and warrants. In general, information is reported opposite the country or geographical area where the foreigner is located, as shown on records of reporting institutions. However, information may not always reflect the ultimate ownership of assets. Reporting institutions are not required to go beyond addresses shown on their records; therefore, they may not be aware of the actual country of domicile of the ultimate debtor or creditor.

Nonbanking Claims and Liabilities

Data on claims and liabilities positions with unaffiliated foreigners are collected quarterly. The data cover such instruments as loans and deposits as well as commercial positions in such instruments as trade payables and receivables. The data are collected from importers and exporters, industrial and commercial concerns, and financial entities such as insurance and pension funds. Data exclude claims on foreigners held by banks in the United States. Historically, the TIC nonbanking reports exclude accounts of nonbanking enterprises in the United States with their own branches and subsidiaries abroad or with their foreign parent companies. Such accounts with foreign affiliates are reported by business enterprises to the Commerce Department on its direct investment forms. There was an exception when reporting of foreign affiliate positions of insurance underwriting subsidiaries and financial intermediaries were included for reports between end-March 2003 and end-March 2006. That reporting requirement was discontinued with the reports beginning as of June 2006. As with the banking data, information in general is reported opposite the country or geographical area where the foreigner is located, as shown on records of reporting institutions. However, information may not always reflect the ultimate ownership of assets. Reporting institutions are not required to go beyond addresses shown on their records; therefore, they may not be aware of the actual country of domicile of the ultimate debtor or creditor.

Derivatives Holdings and Transactions

Data on U.S. resident holdings of, and transactions in, derivatives contracts with foreign residents are collected quarterly by the TIC Form D. The data cover both Over-The-Counter (OTC) contracts and Exchange Traded contracts. The data are collected from banks, securities brokers and dealers, and nonfinancial companies in the U.S. with sizable holdings of derivatives contracts. A derivative contract is a financial contract whose value is derived from the values of one or more underlying assets, reference rates, or indices of asset values or reference rates. Common types of derivatives contracts include forwards, futures, swaps and options. The TIC Form D collects data on derivatives contracts that meet the FASB Statement No. 133 definition. Holdings of derivatives contracts are measured by their fair (market) values, where the fair value is generally defined as the amount for which a derivative contract could be exchanged in a current transaction between willing parties, other than in a forced or liquidation sale. The fair value is different from a derivative's "notional" amount, which is the number of currency units, shares, bushels, pounds, or other units specified in a derivative instrument and used to compute the payouts from the contract. Derivatives contracts are separated and aggregated according to whether, from the perspective of the U.S. resident, a contract's fair value on the last day of the quarter is positive or negative. The gross positive (or negative) fair value is the sum of all derivatives positions with positive (or negative) fair values from the U.S. resident's perspective. The data on U.S. net settlements with foreign residents include all cash receipts and payments made during the quarter for the acquisition, sale, or final closeout of derivatives, including all settlement payments under the terms of derivatives contracts such as the periodic settlement under a swap agreement and the daily settlement of an exchange-traded contract. In calculating net settlements, U.S. receipts of cash from foreign persons are positive amounts (+), and U.S. payments of cash to foreign persons are negative amounts (−). Items excluded from net settlements are: (a) commissions and fees (they are regarded as transactions in financial services rather than as transactions in derivatives); (b) collateral including initial and maintenance margins, whether or not in the form of cash; and (c) purchases of underlying commodities, securities, or other non-cash assets (e.g., the purchase/sale by foreigners of an underlying long-term security is reported in the TIC data on transactions in long-term securities). The gross positive and negative fair values and net settlement payments on derivatives contracts are reported by country based on the residence of the direct foreign counterparty. Positions of foreign customers on U.S. exchanges are reported opposite the country in which the foreign counterparty resides. In the case of U.S. residents' futures contracts on foreign exchanges, the country of the exchange is reported as the country of the foreign counterparty. In the last case where a U.S. resident trades on a foreign exchange, the country information may not always reflect the ownership of the ultimate holder of the risk in the contract.

Securities Holdings

Cross-border holdings of long-term securities (securities with an original term-to-maturity in excess of one year) are measured at market value through security-level surveys (that is, information is reported separately for each security) that collect data from custodians, issuers, and investors. Previously, such surveys were conducted relatively infrequently: surveys of foreign holdings of U.S. securities were conducted about once every five years, beginning in 1974; surveys of U.S. holdings of foreign securities were conducted about once every three or four years, but only beginning in 1994. Beginning in 2002, annual surveys of foreign holdings of U.S. securities are conducted as of end-June on TIC Form SHL/SHLA; beginning in 2003, annual surveys of U.S. holdings of foreign securities are conducted as of end-December on annual TIC Form SHC/SHCA. Because these data on holdings are security-specific, they permit extensive verification and thus are considered highly reliable. But because the data require thorough editing, they are available only after a lag of about one year.

Securities Transactions

The data series are based on submissions of monthly TIC Form S, "Purchases and Sales of Long-Term Securities by Foreigners." These reports are mandatory and are filed by banks, securities dealers, investors, and other entities in the U.S. who deal directly with foreign residents in purchases and sales of long-term securities (equities and debt issues with an original maturity of more than one year) issued by U.S. or foreign-based firms. Typically, the data series are revised for up to 24 months after the initial "as of" reporting date. The data are released to the public with a lag of about 1 1/2 months. The data reflect only those transactions between U.S. residents and counterparties located outside the United States. The data cover transactions in six classifications of securities: There are four domestic types of securities, which include U.S. Treasury bonds and notes, bonds of U.S. government corporations and federally-sponsored agencies, U.S. corporate and other bonds, and U.S. corporate and other stocks; and two foreign types of securities, namely foreign bonds and foreign stocks. The securities data are collected and presented from the perspective of the foreign parties to the transactions. By definition, "gross purchases by foreigners" are gross sales by U.S. residents. Similarly, "gross sales by foreigners" are gross purchases by U.S. residents. As an example, to derive net foreign purchases of U.S. Treasury bonds and notes vis-a-vis a particular country or geographical area, take the difference between the two columns labeled "gross purchases by foreigners of U.S. Treasury bonds and notes" and "gross sales by foreigners of U.S. Treasury bonds and notes." As another example, to derive net U.S. purchases of foreign equities, you would take the difference between "gross purchases by foreigners of foreign stocks" and "gross sales by foreigners of foreign stocks." In each example, a positive difference indicates net foreign purchases from U.S. residents (U.S. capital inflow); a negative difference indicates net foreign sales to U.S. residents (U.S. capital outflow).

What Does the Chart Say?

TIC data has been issued for the past 30 years, but only recently, due to an enormous rise in foreign participation in our markets, has it grabbed the attention of the international financial markets. TIC offers a measure of foreign demand for U.S. debt and assets. The thinking is that strong inflows underpin the value of the dollar since foreigners must purchase dollars in order to buy our securities. Like some of the other economic indicators, most notably NFP, there is certainly a knee-jerk reaction to the release, but Figure 2.4 does not show a consistent relationship between TIC and the DXY. The general trend for TIC since 1970 has been up, but the DXY has rallied and declined during that time. There have been long periods of positive correlation, notably May 1980 to May 1984, July 1999 to February 2003. However, there have also been extended periods of negative correlation, such as November 1984 to October 1987.

PRODUCER AND CONSUMER PRICE INDEXES

The producer price index (PPI) and consumer price index (CPI) are inflation indicators released monthly by the Bureau of Labor Statistics (BLS). Like most U.S. economic indicators, the releases occur at 8:30 A.M. ET. Both are released mid-month but the PPI is released a day before the CPI. The PPI measures the average change over time in the selling prices received by domestic producers of goods and services. The calculation of PPI involves price changes for about 100,000 goods, which are separated into over 10,000 different producer price indexes. PPIs are available for the products of nearly every industry in the mining and manufacturing sectors of the U.S. economy. There are three major categories that the 10,000 indexes fall into: commodity indexes, industry indexes, and stage-of-processing indexes. The stage-of-processing indexes include crude materials, intermediate materials, and finished goods. The finished goods indexes are usually focused on because they are the items that have the greatest impact on the consumer, who is responsible for roughly 70 percent of U.S. GDP.

The CPI is a measure of the average change over time in the prices paid by urban consumers for a market basket of consumer goods and services. There are actually different CPIs for two different population groups. Spending patterns for all urban consumers is referred to as CPI-U; spending patterns for urban wage earners and clerical workers is referred to as CPI-W. Since the former represents 87 percent of the population, analysts focus on CPI-U (which we will refer to as simply CPI). Not included in the CPI are the spending patterns of persons living in rural nonmetropolitan areas, farm families, persons in the Armed Forces, and those in institutions, such as prisons and mental hospitals.

The CPI market basket is developed from detailed expenditure information provided by families and individuals on what they actually bought. About 10,000 families from around the country provide information on their spending habits in a series of quarterly interviews. To collect information on frequently purchased items such as food and personal care products, another 7,500 families keep diaries listing everything they bought during a two-week period. Altogether, more than 30,000 individuals and families provide expenditure information for use in determining the importance, or weight, of the more than 200 categories in the CPI.

BLS data collectors visit or call thousands of retail stores, service establishments, rental units, and so forth, all over the United States to obtain information on the prices of the thousands of items used to track and measure price changes in the CPI. These economic assistants record the prices of about 80,000 items each month representing a scientifically selected sample of the prices paid by consumers for the goods and services purchased. The recorded information is sent to the national office of the BLS where commodity specialists who have detailed knowledge about the particular goods or services and their prices review the data. These specialists check the data for accuracy and consistency and make any necessary corrections or adjustments.

As mentioned, the BLS has classified all expenditure items into more than 200 categories. These 200 categories are arranged into eight major groups:

1. FOOD AND BEVERAGES (breakfast cereal, milk, coffee, chicken, wine, service meals and snacks)
2. HOUSING (rent of primary residence, owners' equivalent rent, fuel oil, bedroom furniture)
3. APPAREL (men's shirts and sweaters, women's dresses, jewelry)
4. TRANSPORTATION (new vehicles, airline fares, gasoline, motor vehicle insurance)
5. MEDICAL CARE (prescription drugs and medical supplies, physicians' services, eyeglasses and eye care, hospital services)
6. RECREATION (televisions, pets and pet products, sports equipment, admissions)
7. EDUCATION AND COMMUNICATION (college tuition, postage, telephone services, computer software and accessories)
8. OTHER GOODS AND SERVICES (tobacco and smoking products, haircuts and other personal services, funeral expenses)

Weights, based on the percentage of income that consumers devote to each group, are given to each of the eight groups in order to calculate the

CPI. "Housing" is the largest group at over 40 percent, while "Other goods and services" and "Apparel" are the lowest at close to 4 percent.

The price collected for an item included in the PPI is the revenue received by its producer. Taxes are not included in the price because they do not represent revenue to the producer. The price collected for an item included in the CPI is the out-of-pocket expenditure by a consumer for the item. Taxes are included in the price because they are necessary expenditures by the consumer for the item. The differences between the PPI and CPI are consistent with the different uses of the two measures. A primary use of the PPI is to deflate revenue streams in order to measure real growth in output. A primary use of the CPI is to adjust income and expenditure streams for changes in the cost of living. Although the PPI and CPI are different in the way they are calculated, they track each other very well, as can be seen in Figures 2.5 and 2.6.

The headline CPI release includes CPI for all goods and services and CPI for all goods and services except food and energy. The index that

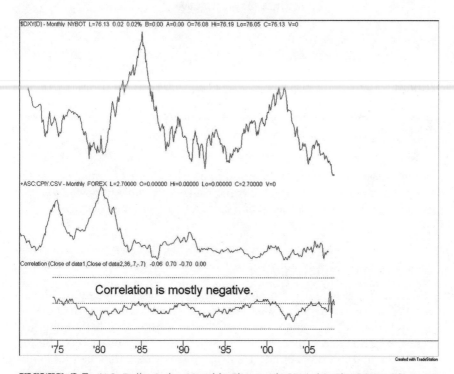

FIGURE 2.5 U.S. Dollar Index Monthly Chart with CPI (y/y): The 36-month correlation between the DXY and CPI y/y is mostly negative
Source: Chart created on TradeStation®, the flagship product of TradeStation Technologies, Inc.

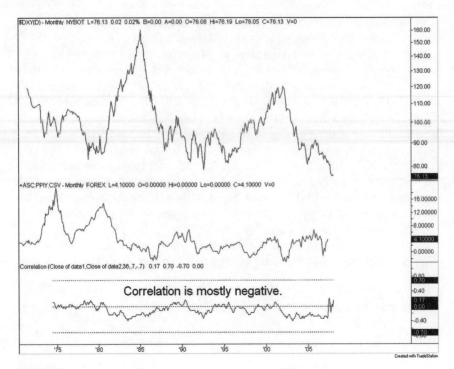

FIGURE 2.6 U.S. Dollar Index Monthly Chart with PPI (y/y): Similar to CPI, the 36-month correlation between the DXY and PPI y/y is mostly negative
Source: Chart created on TradeStation®, the flagship product of TradeStation Technologies, Inc.

excludes food and energy is referred to as *core inflation.* Analysts prefer the index excluding food and energy, because food and energy are volatile components of the index. Removing these components helps analysts more easily detect long-term trends in inflation.

What Does the Chart Say?

The assumption is that increased inflation (higher PPI and CPI readings) is positive for a currency. Most analysts focus on what action the Federal Reserve might or might not take in response to an inflation number. Figure 2.7 shows that there is no consistent correlation between the fed funds rate and the DXY, either. If inflation is elevated, then central banks increase interest rates in order to combat inflation. Higher interest rates can bolster a currency by giving better returns on fixed-income investments. This line of thinking is convincing but incorrect. If it were correct,

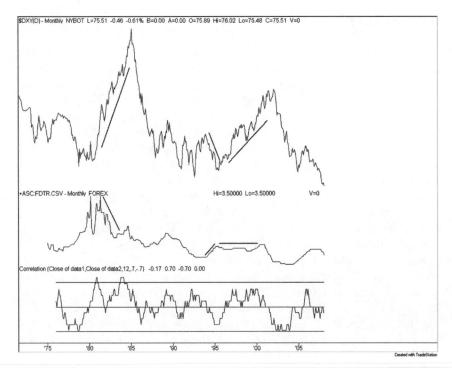

$DXY(D) - Monthly NYBOT L=75.51 -0.46 -0.61% B=0.00 A=0.00 O=75.89 Hi=76.02 Lo=75.48 C=75.51 V=0

+ASC.FDTR.CSV - Monthly FOREX   Hi=3.50000 Lo=3.50000   V=0

Correlation (Close of data1,Close of data2,12,.7,-.7) -0.17 0.70 -0.70 0.00

'75   '80   '85   '90   '95   '00   '05

Created with TradeStation

FIGURE 2.7 There is no consistent correlation between the fed funds rate and the DXY, either
Source: Chart created on TradeStation®, the flagship product of TradeStation Technologies, Inc.

then we would surely see extended periods of positive correlation between inflation indicators such as the PPI and CPI and the DXY, not to mention the fed funds rate and the DXY. Not only are there very few times when a positive correlation exists, but the correlation for the DXY and inflation indicators is actually negative for most of the last 30+ years. There are three specific instances when the fed funds rate and the DXY diverged. In the early 1980s, interest rates fell while the DXY rallied to an all-time high. In 1993 and 1995, the fed funds rate fell while the DXY rallied. From 1995 to 2000, the fed funds rate fell slightly while the DXY rallied significantly.

If you stop and think about what inflation really is, then the negative correlation makes sense. *Inflation* is an increase in the money supply, which leads to currency devaluation. If there are more dollars, then each dollar is worth less than what it previously was worth.

CONCLUSION

I am not blind to the fact that market moves can be considerable and violent in the minutes following an economic release. However, trading during these times is far from strategically optimal. For one, liquidity is at a premium during these times which makes it difficult to enter and exit a trade at will. A common problem that news traders face is slippage. For example, even if a trader is on the correct side of the trade for the initial knee-jerk reaction following the news release, there is no guarantee that the trader will be able to exit the position due to a fast moving market. In an even worst-case scenario, a trader may find that price gaps over his or her stop order following the news release, resulting in a much larger loss than planned.

The risk of additional costs to the trader increases significantly during news release times. If you are looking for an adrenaline high, then scalping news-driven price action is for you. If your goal is to make money by trading the FX market intelligently, then I believe that this book can help you develop a better approach. Trading is difficult enough, so why subject yourself to an increased risk of failure. The crowd loves this kind of trading because it provides instant excitement. More often than not, a price is paid for that excitement in the form of a losing trade. Las Vegas provides instant excitement and on balance people lose there as well; at least the casinos are nice enough to offer free drinks.

CHAPTER 3

The Power of
Magazine Covers

You are probably asking yourself, "What is a chapter on magazine covers doing in a book about currency trading?" Magazine covers are one of the best indicators of mass psychology and, by extension, one of the best signals that a market is close to forming a significant top or bottom. Markets, like life in general, are not linear. Markets change direction and bullish (optimism) for a top and bearish (pessimism) for a bottom—extreme sentiment—is required to effect that change. A major magazine would not devote its cover story to a financial market unless the story in question was considered newsworthy. A story (especially one about the value of a currency) is not considered newsworthy to a major magazine unless the public is obsessed with the story, and an obsessed public defines extreme sentiment. Since sentiment extremes accompany market turns, by association, major magazine covers are contrarian indicators and signal market turns.

The idea that magazine covers can be used as contrarian indicators in financial markets is not new. Paul Montgomery of Universal Economics has studied the covers of major news magazines for years and found that when a magazine's cover takes a directional stand on the stock market, that market usually forms a significant top (if the cover is bullish) or bottom (if the cover is bearish). The same concept can be applied to the foreign exchange market.

THE DEATH OF EQUITIES—AUGUST 13, 1979

One of the most famous "magazine cover indicator" examples is the August 13, 1979, issue of *Business Week*. The cover story was titled "The Death of Equities." Crashed paper airplanes, made from stock certificates, were pictured on the cover. The gist of the article was that little hope existed for stocks. Inflation was rampant, and it was assumed that this would remain the case. For this reason, gold and even diamonds were being touted as much better investments than stocks. In fact, the Labor Department had just passed a law allowing pension funds to invest in asset classes other than the stock and bond markets, among them hard assets such as gold. Of course, gold topped out at $873 in January 1980 and just recently reached that level again—over 27 years later. An excerpt from the article describes the mood of the day regarding the U.S. stock market.

> *Even if the economic climate could be made right again for equity investment, it would take another massive promotional campaign to bring people back into the market. Yet the range of investment opportunities is so much wider now than in the 1950s that it is unlikely that the experience of two decades ago, when the number of equity investors increased by 250% in 15 years, could be repeated. For better or for worse, then, the U.S. economy probably has to regard the death of equities as a near-permanent condition, reversible some day, but not soon.* [1]

The month that this article was written the Dow closed at 887.63 and bottomed at 729.95 seven months later before the bull market of the 1980s and 1990s drove the Dow over 1,000 percent higher (see Figure 3.1). The point here is not to single out *Business Week* for its shoddy investment advice, but to illustrate that the mainstream financial media tends to *describe* what has happened rather than *forecast* what will happen. The end result is that they are wrong at the worst possible time, whether that is being bearish at the bottom or bullish at the top.

MAGAZINE COVERS IN THE CURRENCY MARKET

Following the collapse of the Bretton Woods system in 1971, exchange rates were allowed to fluctuate and multinational banks began speculating in the new market. With speculation came emotion, principally fear, greed,

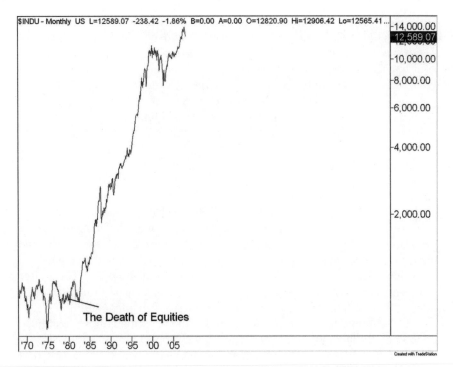

$INDU - Monthly US L=12589.07 -238.42 -1.86% B=0.00 A=0.00 O=12820.90 Hi=12906.42 Lo=12565.41 ...

14,000.00
12,589.07
10,000.00
8,000.00
6,000.00
4,000.00
2,000.00

The Death of Equities

'70 '75 '80 '85 '90 '95 '00 '05

Created with TradeStation

FIGURE 0.1 The infamous Death of Equities cover from *Business Week* appears on newsstands just before the great equity bull market of the 1980s and 1990s
Source: Chart created on TradeStation®, the flagship product of TradeStation Technologies, Inc.

hope, and the wild swings from optimism and pessimism that can be seen in any freely traded market. In June 1971, the synthetic U.S. dollar index (the actual index has been around since 1973 and the DXY [USD Index] has traded exclusively on the New York Board of Trade [NYBOT] since 1985) traded just above 119.00 but by October 1978, the index had plummeted to just above 82.00. Our look at the history of the magazine indicator in FX begins with the November 13, 1978, issue of *Time*.

To the Rescue—November 13, 1978

George Washington's portrait, the one that appears on the dollar bill, was featured on the November 13, 1978, issue of *Time*. However, the portrait included a white bandage above his right eye and a blackened left eye. The implications of course were that the dollar was beaten up. In truth, the dollar was in shambles. From October 1976 to October 1978, the buck had fallen just over 40 percent against the German mark (the euro was established in 1999 . . . more on that later). The psychological environment regarding the dollar and the U.S. economy couldn't have been much worse; equities had traded sideways for over a decade, and inflation was out of control (the prime rate was at 10.75 percent). The cover story, "To Rescue the Dollar," stated that "the plunge in the value of the dollar posed a gigantic threat to the stability of the whole world financial system."[2]

Then President Carter put together a "dollar rescue plan that amounts to a sharp and startling reversal of previous policies and aims to restore credibility to America's currency."[3] The basic plan was to raise the discount rate by one full point (the largest increase in 45 years), reduce by $3 billion the funds that U.S. banks have available to lend, intervene in the currency market by borrowing $30 billion of foreign currencies to buy back U.S. dollars, and significantly increase U.S. sales of gold. An excerpt from the article explains that "the practical aim of these steps is to break the deadly circle in which inflation devalues the dollar, which in turn pushes up the prices of imported goods, which in turn worsens inflation." The writer of this article clearly understood the psychological aspect adding that "like many governmental economic steps, this is a *psychological* action."

Government interventions, such as the one described above, will have an impact initially but a change in the market's psychological landscape is required in order to trigger a longer-term change in trend. The image of a beat-up dollar (George Washington) on the cover of *Time*, a magazine more renowned for its coverage of political events, celebrities, and pop culture, signaled that change in trend. The pessimistic extreme had been reached. The dollar index doubled (100 percent gain) in less than seven years, which brings us to 1985. See Figure 3.2.

Petropanic and the Pound—February 2, 1985

Appearing on the top right-hand corner of the February 2, 1985, *The Economist* cover was "Petropanic and the Pound." This was not the main cover story, but the editors felt that the ultra-depressed level of the British pound was newsworthy enough for at least a portion of the cover. The GBPUSD exchange rate closed the week of February 1, 1985, at 1.1110. Weakness was attributed to the falling price of oil. In the words of *The Economist*, "Sterling is a petrocurrency whose exchange rate is affected by Iranian mullahs, OPEC talks, and the logical pressure of market forces in a world that needs a third less oil to produce a dollar of output than it did 12 years ago. But several other countries rely more on their oil wealth than Britain does, and their currencies have not fallen so much."[4]

Whether the writer of this article knew it or not, he was hinting that oil was not as big a factor in the pound exchange rate as previously thought. By mentioning that "other countries rely more on their oil wealth than

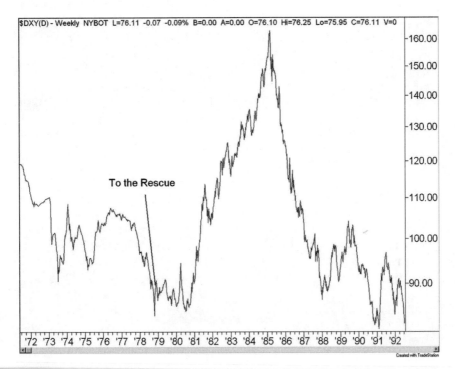

$DXY(D) - Weekly NYBOT L=76.11 -0.07 -0.09% B=0.00 A=0.00 O=76.10 Hi=76.25 Lo=75.95 C=76.11 V=0

To the Rescue

FIGURE 3.2 The USD was in deep trouble and in need of "rescue" in November 1978, at least according to *Time*
Source: Chart created on TradeStation®, the flagship product of TradeStation Technologies, Inc.

Britain does, and their currencies have not fallen so much," the writer is acknowledging that something else is at work in the market—sentiment. Regardless of the reasons cited for the plummet of the British pound, *The Economist*'s granting cover space to the value of the British pound signaled that sentiment regarding the pound was about as bearish as possible, and that a turn was due.

As it happened, the GBPUSD found a bottom four weeks later at 1.0520 and has yet to look back (see Figure 3.3). On the other side of the British pound trade was the U.S. dollar. Another cover story dedicated to the greenback, this time with bullish imagery, was on newsstands one month later.

Superdollar Overdoes It—March 2, 1985

Just four weeks after the "Petropanic and the Pound" article, the image of Superman with a dollar sign on his chest graced the cover of *The*

FIGURE 3.3 *The Economist*'s acknowledgment of panic regarding the devaluation of the British pound was one of the great buy signals of all time in FX
Source: Chart created on TradeStation®, the flagship product of TradeStation Technologies, Inc.

Economist. The title of the cover story, "Superdollar Overdoes It" implied that the dollar was overvalued. However, the value of the magazine indicator is based on the idea that sentiment extremes occur at major turning points. A bullish trend featured as a cover story signals an optimism extreme. In other words, there is no more buying power because everyone who would buy has already bought. Therefore, a correction of this extreme, if not an outright reversal of trend, is inevitable.

This cover story is also an example of what Elliott Wave International describes as the "uh-oh effect." In short, "the uh-oh effect is a brief point of recognition at the very end of a long rise when some participants glimpse the enormous potential for a devastating reversal. Bubble references appear to be an extension of this vague sense of peril to the social realm except that, after so many years of frenzied price advances, users have lost respect for the meaning of the word bubble, which is a speculative scheme that comes to nothing."[5]

FIGURE 3.4 *The Economist's* "Superdollar Overdoes It" cover appears at the DXY all-time high

Source: Chart created on TradeStation®, the flagship product of TradeStation Technologies, Inc.

This was the March 2, 1985, issue. March 2 was a Saturday, and the U.S. dollar index made its all-time high during the week that ended March 1st. Three years later, the greenback had fallen from just below 165.00 to below 90.00. See Figure 3.4.

Euroshambles—September 16, 2000

The Eurozone was established with the launch of the euro on January 1, 1999, and the EURUSD opened at 1.1673 that Sunday evening. The exchange rate declined for the first 6 months and for 18 of the first 22 months. By September 16, 2000, the EURUSD had fallen below .8600, a decline of 27 percent. The September 16, 2000, issue of *The Economist* was the signal to cover short positions and enter into long positions.

That issue of *The Economist* featured the economic problems that the newly established single currency area known as the Eurozone was facing.

The cover, a black background, was of the reading of a car's gas tank on empty and in big white letters above the image was "Euroshambles." The empty gas tank symbolized perfectly the state of mind regarding the euro at that time. The currency was running on empty, and the EURUSD was at an all-time low (taking into consideration synthetic DEM rates, the all-time low was actually in February 1985 at .7155), closing on September 15th at .8532. The first paragraph of the cover story reads,

> *The echoes from the 1970s and 1980s are becoming oppressive. Oil crises, fuel shortages, street blockades and protests, currency woes, paralyzed governments, excessive taxes: to many observers, both within and beyond Europe, it must seem as if the old continent is once again locked in the grip of its old disease, eurosclerosis, which first struck a quarter of a century ago, just after the 1973 oil shock. Was all the promise of Europe's single market and its new currency, coupled with the oft talked-of spread of Thatcherite supply-side reforms across the continent, just an illusion?[6]*

This lead paragraph captures the pessimistic sentiment that permeated the minds of traders and investors at that time regarding the euro. The article later read, "Many voices are now proclaiming that the single currency has 'failed' and that Europe's sickly economies are doomed to be left behind by a resurgent America—and they do not come only from hardened British Eurosceptics. Recent polls suggest that support for the euro has sunk to new lows in Germany, and the Danish referendum that is being held later this month on whether to join the euro now rests on a knife-edge."[7]

Another article in the same issue, titled "Europe's Economies— Stumbling Yet Again?," mentioned that, "Newspaper headlines are fretting about the fact that the euro has fallen to a 'record low' of below 86 cents, 27% below its starting level in January 1999. Some dealers predict that it could soon hit 80 cents, even though it is already well below most estimates of its fair value."[8]

Does the environment described in these articles sound like one that is euro bullish? Of course not. Even the professionals (the dealers) were predicting 80 cents. Of course, the EURUSD found a bottom in the week that ended October 27, 2000, at .8225, six weeks after the cover of *The Economist* read "Euroshambles." The rate challenged .9600 three months later, consolidated for a year, and then rallied nearly 5,000 pips in three years. (See Figure 3.5.) Interestingly, the most timely signal to exit euro longs would come in future magazine covers proclaiming the demise of the U.S. dollar.

FIGURE 3.5 Buying the Euro when it was in "shambles" would have been quite the trade
Source: Chart created on TradeStation®, the flagship product of TradeStation Technologies, Inc.

Let the Dollar Drop—February 7, 2004

The week that the "Euroshambles" cover came to newsstands, the EURUSD closed at .8529. By the time the February 7, 2004, issue of *The Economist* was released, the EURUSD was trading at 1.2690. The environment now was the exact opposite as it was in 2000 (when the bearish euro cover came to newsstands). Dollar bears and euro bulls were jumping on the bandwagon in the same manner that dollar bulls and euro bears had just four years earlier. From cover story to cover story, the EURUSD gained 49 percent.

The lead story from the February 7, 2004, issue was titled "Let the Dollar Drop." The subtitle was "Some think the dollar has fallen too far. On the contrary, it has not fallen by enough." Speculators could have used this cover as a short-term topping signal. The EURUSD closed the week of February 6 at 1.2690 and at 1.2735 the next week. Twelve weeks after the

FIGURE 3.6 The DXY rallied significantly (EURUSD falling) in the months after the "Let the Dollar Drop" cover appeared
Source: Chart created on TradeStation®, the flagship product of TradeStation Technologies, Inc.

release of the bearish dollar cover, the EURUSD closed at 1.1977, not an immaterial move. See Figure 3.6.

The article was written just prior to the G7 meeting in Boca Raton, Florida. The currency trading world was speculating as to whether or not governments would act together to curtail the dollar's decline. As it happened, there was no such talk from the meeting about putting an end to the dollar's decline, but the dollar rallied anyway. Why? Mood was so pessimistic regarding the buck at that point that it was simply time for it to rally. The article mentions that "the euro has risen by 50% against the dollar since July 2001"[9] and that "a new agreement on exchange rates at this weekend's meeting seems unlikely given that the G7 members have such different goals."[10] This is true, but a speculator needs to be concerned first with *future* direction of the market, not with what has *already* happened. This sounds obvious, but most of the financial media, as well as a great many traders, tend to extrapolate trends. In other words, they describe what has just happened and imply that this will continue to happen.

In this case, the magazine cover signaled that the dollar was about to put in a bottom, at least temporarily. The dollar did decline following its brief rally to just below EURUSD 1.2000. By December 2004, the greenback was pressing 1.3500 EURUSD, a roughly 5 percent drop from the February 2004 dollar bearish cover story (a small setback compared with the nearly 50 percent EURUSD rally from the euro bearish cover story). Yet another dollar bearish feature in December 2004 signaled that 2005 was setting up for dollar bulls and euro bears.

The Disappearing Dollar—December 3, 2004

For the week that ended on December 3, 2004, the EURUSD closed at 1.3457. Dollar bulls found themselves in a precarious position, but there was reason for optimism as the cover from the December 4, 2004, issue of *The Economist* made it quite clear that conditions were ripe for a dollar bottom (EURUSD top). The cover story, titled "The Disappearing Dollar," contains this excerpt in its second paragraph. "America has habits that are inappropriate, to say the least, for the guardian of the world's main reserve currency: rampant government borrowing, furious consumer spending and a current account deficit big enough to have bankrupted any other country some time ago. This makes a dollar devaluation inevitable . . . why would anybody want to invest in a currency that will almost certainly depreciate?"[11]

The last sentence demonstrates the extrapolating that the financial media makes a habit of doing. The EURUSD had appreciated 60 percent (from .8500 to 1.3500) in four years, and this article is making a dollar bearish argument *now*? *The Economist* was confident in its dollar bearish position as well. These sentences appeared later in the article. "The dollar now seems likely to fall further" and "over the next few years it seems an excellent bet that there will be a large drop in the dollar."

"The Disappearing Dollar" article was hardly an outlook for the world's reserve currency, but rather an explanation of what had already happened and what everyone already knew. That is, the dollar had been plummeting. This article signaled the end of the EURUSD bull run. The boat, full of dollar bears, tipped over. Four weeks following the December 4 issue, the EURUSD peaked at 1.3666 and plunged 15 percent in 11 months. Selling dollars in 2005 was hardly "an excellent bet." See Figure 3.7.

The Sadness of Japan—February 16, 2002

A similar situation was going on regarding the Japanese yen in February 2002. From November 1999 to February 2002, the USDJPY had skyrocketed from just above 101.00 to just over 135.00. (For those unfamiliar with

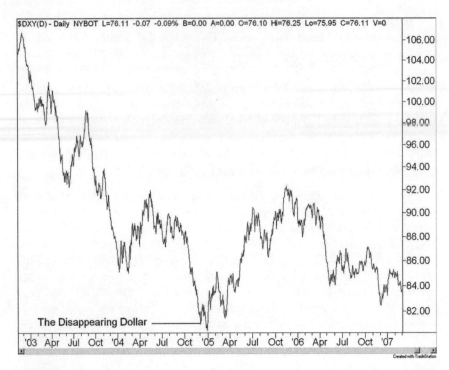

FIGURE 3.7 "The Disappearing Dollar" cover preceded the largest rally in the DXY in years
Source: Chart created on TradeStation®, the flagship product of TradeStation Technologies, Inc.

the nature of exchange rates, the first currency in the pair is known as the base currency, and the second currency is known as the counter currency. In this example, the USD is the base currency and the JPY is the counter currency. When the exchange rate rises, the counter currency is decreasing in value relative to the base currency. In other words, a USDJPY rally means that the JPY is weakening.)

The JPY was at two-and-a-half-year lows against the USD and, according to the financial media, the outlook was bleak. The cover story for the February 16, 2002, issue of *The Economist* was titled, "The Sadness of Japan." Here is an excerpt from the lead article of that issue.

> *There is no single solution to Japan's ills: neither a depreciating yen, not monetary expansion by the bank of Japan, not nationalism of the banks (it goes on) . . . will bring Japan's economy leaping back to productive life. The government needs to do all of these, over a*

period of years, in order to reflate demand as well as reinvigorating enterprise and restoring consumers' confidence. All measures will be painful, in their different ways.[12]

According to this article, the yen had to depreciate more and it was going to "be painful." Not only did the yen not depreciate, it appreciated—a lot. The USDJPY rate topped out two weeks before the article was released at 135.14. The week that the article was released, the pair rallied to 135.01; three weeks later the USDJPY had dropped below 127.00. Five months later, the rate dropped below 116.00. The decline continued until January 2005, when the USDJPY found a bottom at 101.68. See Figure 3.8.

An Economy Singed—June 22, 2002

The next example is not related to exchange rates but does express the mood that accompanies market bottoms. U.S. equities had been

FIGURE 3.8 "The Sadness of Japan" cover timed buying the JPY (selling the USDJPY) to the week
Source: Chart created on TradeStation®, the flagship product of TradeStation Technologies, Inc.

plummeting since the "bubble" burst in early 2000. The Dow Jones Industrial Average had lost 22 percent of its value by June 21, 2002, and the S&P 500 Index had declined over 37 percent from its March 2000 high. One of the largest financial bubbles in history had burst, and most market participants expected stock markets to continue sliding for a while longer. The financial landscape and mentality of investors was described by *The Economist* in its June 22, 2002, issue. The cover of this issue was of a burning $100 bill, in the shape of the United States, and the title on the cover was "An Economy Singed." Here is an excerpt from the lead article of that issue:

> *Certainly as far as investors are concerned, the much-touted American model has lost a lot of its allure. They are fretting over several potential economic weaknesses, and also over continuing revelations of corporate America's shoddy accounting, greedy managers and lousy investment decisions—and they are selling. The results are clear. For the first time since the 1920s, stock markets have been falling during the first few months of an economic recovery. The Dow Jones Industrial Average has fallen in ten of the past 13 weeks, and is now down to the levels of early 1999.*[13]

This passage would make you think that American capitalism would not exist much longer. The mention of the 1920s, which saw the stock market crash of 1929, does not exactly conjure up bullish images. Additional commentary from that issue mentions that "with no evidence of a rebound in investment, any hint of a flagging consumer suggests that the recovery will be weak at best, and certainly not the robust boom that markets counted on at the start of the year."[14] Another article from the same issue states that "now should be the time for stock markets to roar ahead again. Instead, share prices continue to slip" and that "the bull market wisdom of always buying 'on the dips' might seem to apply. Yet this summer—and possibly for some seasons to come—the wisdom may not be borne out."[15]

One "reason" for staying away from equities, according to this article, was "sluggish profits." The writer later exclaims that "profits are at the front of investors' minds" and that "firms are finding that corporate profits are rising rather more slowly, if at all." The contrarian knows that profits are not at the front of investors' minds—fear is. A bearish magazine cover is the sign that selling is, or is close to, over. The DJIA and the S&P 500 made short-term lows one month later, at the end of July. The longer-term lows were put in toward the beginning of October. The DJIA went on to surpass its January 2000 high of 11749.97 by over 2000 points a little less than five years after this article was published. See Figures 3.9 and 3.10.

FIGURE 3.9 The "An Economy Singed" cover signaled the best buying opportunity for equities since "The Death of Equities" cover nearly 25 years earlier. The Dow went to new highs just 5 years later
Source: Chart created on TradeStation®, the flagship product of TradeStation Technologies, Inc.

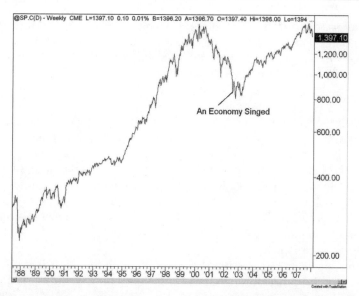

FIGURE 3.10 Similarly, the S&P went to a new high (slightly) five years later
Source: Chart created on TradeStation®, the flagship product of TradeStation Technologies, Inc.

The subtitle for the lead article, "An Economy Singed," was "The markets' mood reflects a poor outlook for America's economy." A more accurate subtitle would have been "The markets' mood indicates that stock markets are close to a significant bottom."

It is December 2007 as I write this book and the EURUSD hit a high of 1.4967 on November 23. Guess what? The December 1 issue of *The Economist* features the U.S. dollar yet again. An image of George Washington in an airplane that is going down in flames is on the cover with the title, "The panic about the dollar." The day that this cover hit newsstands, the EURUSD rate closed at 1.4744 in New York dealing. Today is December 20 and the EURUSD is over 400 pips lower at 1.4322. This most recent cover preceded the largest dollar rally (against the euro) in nearly three years. Coincidence? I think not.

CONCLUSION

The examples above are a few of the many contrarian signals in financial markets that magazine covers have provided. In 2007, a group of professors from the University of Richmond, Virginia, conducted a study in order to determine whether positive cover stories are associated with superior future performance and whether negative stories are associated with inferior future performance regarding specific corporations. "Superior and inferior were determined in comparison with an index or another company in the same industry and of the same size." Over 2,000 cover stories were compiled from *Business Week, Fortune,* and *Forbes* over a 20-year period (1982–2002) and divided into five categories: 1 for definitely positive, 2 for positive/optimistic, 3 for neutral, 4 for negative, and 5 for definitely negative. Of the 2,080 cover stories, 549 focused on a specific corporation. Of the 549 stories, 350 were definitely positive and 100 were definitely negative. This is almost certainly due to the fact that the 1982–2002 period was a bull market for stocks. The professors found that "positive feature stories headlined on business magazine covers follow extremely positive company performance and negative headlines follow extremely negative performance. In both cases, however, the appearance on a cover of *Business Week, Fortune,* or *Forbes* tends to signal the end of the extreme performance."[16]

The specific examples that I cited along with the statistical tests performed by the professors from the University of Virginia are proof that market turns are a result of sentiment, not news. It is important to understand though that the tops and bottoms are of different degrees. For example, the "To the Rescue" and "Superdollar Overdoes It" articles led to multiyear turns. The more recent magazine covers dedicated to the greenback such as the December 2, 2006, issue of *The Economist* titled "The Falling Dollar" have led to less significant turns, but turns nonetheless. "The Falling Dollar" signal led to just a 500 pip decline in the EURUSD. Like some of the other bigger picture signals that I'll address, magazine covers are an alert that conditions are ripe for a turn. Discipline and money management are still paramount to success.

The magazine cover is the result of a sentiment extreme, which is expressed through other media outlets as well. The number of articles about a financial asset, currencies in our case, will reach its peak at the turn. Google has developed (and is improving) Google Trends, which aims to provide insights into broad search patterns. The URL for the site is http://www.google.com/trends. Type in a topic to see the news reference volume over time. News reference volume is the number of times the topic appeared in Google News stories. Unfortunately, the service is in its early stages and is not yet in real time, but this is additional proof that sentiment extremes lead to market turns. A search for "weak dollar" shows that news stories about the weak dollar peaked in December 2004 and late November 2006. The Dollar Index made multimonth lows in December 2004 and early December 2006. Figure 3.11 shows the results for the Google Trends search for "weak dollar" and Figure 3.12 shows a chart of the Dollar Index.

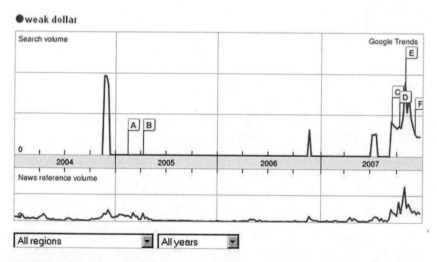

FIGURE 3.11 Peaks in search volume and news reference volume for "weak dollar" occur at DXY bottoms

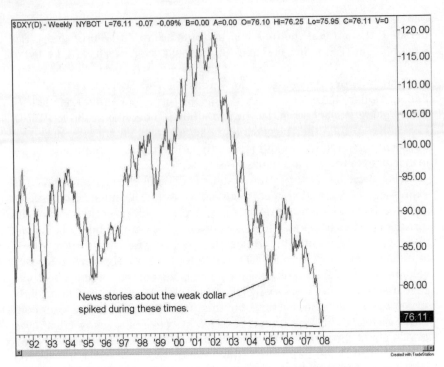

FIGURE 3.12 News about the "weak dollar" spiked in late 2004 (major DXY bottom) and late 2007. (It is too early to tell if this is a significant bottom.)
Source: Chart created on TradeStation®, the flagship product of TradeStation Technologies, Inc.

News headlines at major turns always extrapolate the current trend. Figures 3.13 to 3.16 show a few news headlines that I collected in December 2004 (a significant USD low) and November 2005 (a significant USD top) along with a chart of the corresponding currency.

Like the public, the media is always wrong about the direction of financial markets at the turn. Robert Prechter describes why in *The Wave Principle of Human Social Behavior*:

> *Reporters are usually nonprofessional in the fields that they cover, so the feelings of reporters in general mirror those of the public. Reporters often contact financial analysts who express their own feelings about markets, thus reflecting society's consensus feelings. A bullish analyst rarely gets a forum at a major market bottom, and a bear rarely gets one at a major market top. The media's choice of times to quote certain professionals typically shows those professionals retrospectively in their worst light.*[17]

FIGURE 3.13 Dollar Drops Versus Yen as Japan May Let Currency Strengthen (Bloomberg. December 31, 2004)
Source: Chart created on TradeStation®, the flagship product of TradeStation Technologies, Inc.

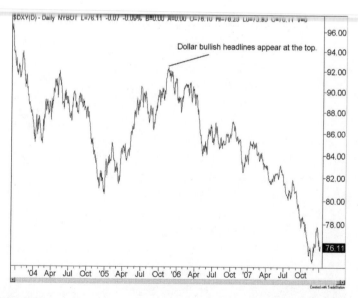

FIGURE 3.14 Dollar Rises as Foreign Buying of U.S. Assets Surges to Record (Bloomberg, November 14, 2005) and Traders Are Most Bullish on Dollar in Five Months (Bloomberg, November 16, 2005)
Source: Chart created on TradeStation®, the flagship product of TradeStation Technologies, Inc.

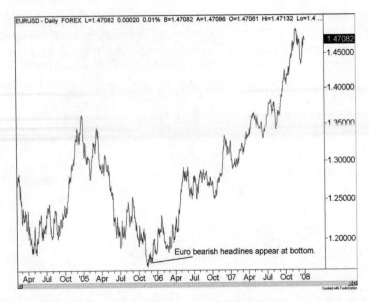

FIGURE 3.15 Euro Likely to Decline as ECB Signals Limit to Rate Increases (Bloomberg, November 28, 2005)
Source: Chart created on TradeStation®, the flagship product of TradeStation Technologies, Inc.

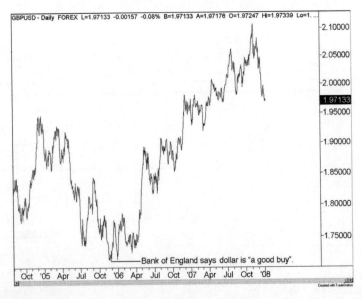

FIGURE 3.16 Bank of England Says Dollar Looks Like a Good Buy (Bloomberg, November 28, 2005)
Source: Chart created on TradeStation®, the flagship product of TradeStation Technologies, Inc.

In other words, the media has to be wrong at the turn, just like the public. The two basic emotions in financial speculation are fear and hope. When one of these emotions overwhelms the other, hope at a top and fear at a bottom, it is only a matter of time until the market turns the other way. Chapter 4 expands on how to use the financial media to provide shorter-term trading signals.

Using News Headlines to Generate Signals

T he magazine indicator is powerful, but rare. The rareness of course contributes to the powerfulness of the indicator. However, traders want action and cannot afford to wait for a magazine cover to help them make a trading decision. More importantly, even though every magazine cover featuring a financial trend results in a reversal of some degree, every reversal is not accompanied by a magazine cover that features a financial trend. The magazine cover indicator works as a contrarian indicator because of mob psychology. Magazines are in the business of selling magazines, so editors are going to feature on the cover what the crowd is obsessed with at the time. In financial markets; the trend reverses once everyone catches on to it. Using the same logic, the financial media provides contrarian signals through other mediums.

Grant Noble wrote a 1989 article for *Stocks & Commodities* magazine titled "The Best Trading Indicator—The Media." He wrote,

> *I believe there is a market sentiment indicator that is more accurate, timely and better able to give long-term predications. The American media gives you three indicators:*
>
> *Long-term. The "popular press" (such as* Time, Newsweek *and the TV networks) normally have major front page articles on financial markets at the top or bottom of long-term market moves of many years. Then they go back to Madonna...*
>
> *Intermediate. The business weeklies (Barron's, Forbes, Business Week) are great indicators of the next three months. Barron's in August 1987 had a bull running away from frantic investors with*

*the caption, "Is the bull leaving you behind?" Right at the top, of
course.*

Short-term. The business section of the New York Times *and the
regular features of the* Wall Street Journal *(especially the futures section) are great short-term indicators. Their front pages also are excellent intermediate indicators.*[1]

We have seen the power of magazine covers and business weeklies,
but I had not thought about tapping into the *Wall Street Journal* pages for
short-term contrary signals. Noble says there is an art to it, but "once you
get the hang of it, it will be must reading." He points out that "extreme language is the key." Three of the more extreme words that you find in headlines of financial periodicals all the time are *surge, plummet,* and *plunge.*
So, I went to the Science, Industry, and Business branch of the New York
Public Library to search the databases for headlines that included

- "dollar" and "surge"
- "dollar" and "plummet"
- "dollar" and "plunge"

After going through hundreds of headlines and noting the dates that
the headlines appeared on the chart, I became a believer in this method
for finding short-term contrarian signals. The headlines are numbered, and
numbers are placed on charts in Figures 4.1 through 4.5 to show where
the headlines actually appeared. (Note: The counter currency [second currency in the pair] strengthens relative to the base currency [first currency
in the pair] when the pair declines and rallies when the pair advances.)

The "Dollar" and "Surge" Search

1. Headline: In a Dollar Selloff, Yen Surges, *Wall Street Journal*, September 8, 2007
   Commentary: September 8th was a Saturday but on the 7th, the
   USDJPY closed at 113.37. Just over a month later, the yen had actually
   declined against the U.S. dollar (USDJPY was at 117.60).

2. Headline: Dollar Surges on the Euro Amid ECB Cash Infusions, *Wall
   Street Journal*, August 14, 2007
   Commentary: The EURUSD closed at 1.3533 on the 14th and at
   1.3425 on the 16th before rallying to 1.4967 in a little over three months.

3. Headline: Yen Surges Against Euro, Dollar, *Wall Street Journal*, February 6, 2007
   Commentary: The USDJPY closed at 120.09 on the 6th and rallied
   200 pips four days later.

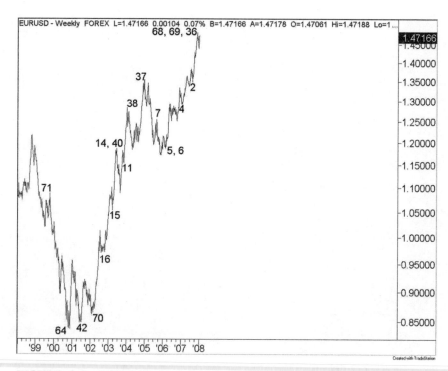

FIGURE 4.1 EURUSD Weekly Bars with Articles Denoted By Numbers
Source: Chart created on TradeStation®, the flagship product of TradeStation Technologies, Inc.

4. Headline: Dollar Surges on Euro, but Ends Mixed, *Wall Street Journal*, January 5, 2007

   Commentary: The EURUSD closed at 1.3007 on the 5th and at 1.2918 on the 12th before embarking on a rally to 1.3650 over the next three months.

5. Headline: Dollar Surges on Data, Outlook of Rate Increase, *Wall Street Journal*, March 24, 2006

   Commentary: The EURUSD closed at 1.1951 on the 24th. The pair was just shy of 1.3000 just two months later.

6. Headline: Dollar Surges Against Euro, Yen On Hints of More Fed Rate Lifts, *Wall Street Journal*, September 28, 2005

   Commentary: The EURUSD closed at 1.2072 on the 27th before dropping over 400 pips in two weeks.

7. Headline: Dollar-Crash Tie To Surge in Yields Rebutted by Fed, *Wall Street Journal*, August 11, 2005

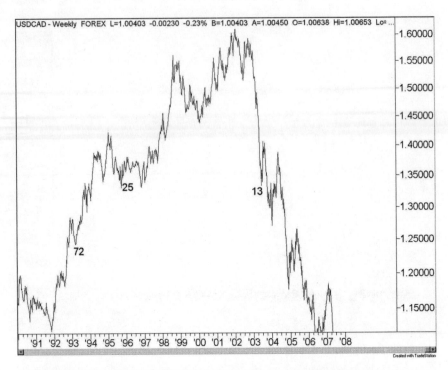

FIGURE 4.2 USDCAD Weekly Bars with Articles Denoted By Numbers
Source: Chart created on TradeStation®, the flagship product of TradeStation Technologies, Inc.

　　　　Commentary: In this headline, surge applies to yields, but notice the "crash" to describe the U.S. dollar. The EURUSD closed at 1.2470 on the 11th and dropped over 300 pips within the next six days.

8. Headline: As the Yen Surges, Tokyo Remains On the Sidelines, *Wall Street Journal*, November 26, 2004
　　　　Commentary: It turned out that this was a major bottom. The USDJPY closed at 102.58 on the 26th. The pair rallied through 106.00 one month later before making a final low at 101.67 on January 17, 2005.

9. Headline: Dollar Finishes Mostly Lower, But Surges Against the Pound, *Wall Street Journal*, May 12, 2004
　　　　Commentary: The GBPUSD closed at 1.7725 on the 12th and made a low on the 14th, closing that day at 1.7606. The GBPUSD was at 1.8600 just two months later.

10. Headline: Yen Jumps to Four-Year High; Rosy outlook in Japan fuels the surge against the dollar. Euro rises as a key rate holds steady, *Los Angeles Times*, April 2, 2004

FIGURE 4.3 USDJPY Weekly Bars with Articles Denoted By Numbers
Source: Chart created on TradeStation®, the flagship product of TradeStation Technologies, Inc.

Commentary: The low in the USDJPY was actually put in two days before this headline hit newswires on March 31st at 103.38. The USDJPY rallied over 1,000 pips in a little over two months.

11. Headline: Dollar Surges Against Counterparts; Upbeat Reports on Economy Spur the Rally in Currency, *Wall Street Journal*, November 4, 2003

    Commentary: The EURUSD closed at 1.1496 on the 4th and made a low at 1.1377 on the 7th before rallying to 1.2750 in two months.

12. Headline: Dollar Surges Against Rivals On Upbeat Greenspan Comments, *Wall Street Journal*, July 16, 2003

    Commentary: This signaled a short-term low. The EURUSD made a low at 1.1113 on the 16th and rallied through 1.1400 on the 25th.

13. Headline: As Canada's Dollar Surges, the Country's Exporters Pay a Steep Price, *Wall Street Journal*, June 24, 2003

    Commentary: A rare USDCAD headline. The pair had actually put in a short-term low at 1.3309 on the 16th and closed at 1.3600 the day

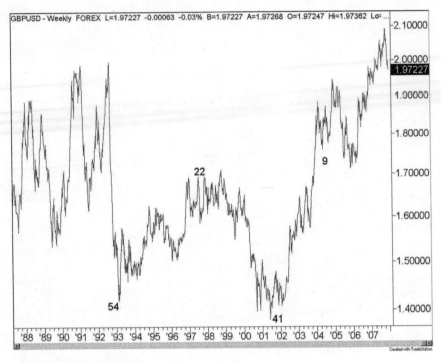

FIGURE 4.4 GBPUSD Weekly Bars with Articles Denoted By Numbers
Source: Chart created on TradeStation®, the flagship product of TradeStation Technologies, Inc.

that this headline was out. The USDCAD rallied to 1.4185 one month later.

14. Headline: U.S. Dollar's Slide Could Push Europe Closer to a Recession, *Wall Street Journal*, May 20, 2003

    Commentary: A bearish USD headline with some hysterics. The EURUSD closed at 1.1734 the day that this headline was published but the pair was below 1.0900 by September.

15. Headline: Dollar Surges Against Rivals As Traders' Optimism Returns, *Wall Street Journal*, April 3, 2003

    Commentary: This U.S. dollar surge article came just after the EURUSD had put in a low at 1.0530 on March 21st. The pair closed at 1.0764 on April 3rd and was above 1.1800 by the end of May.

16. Headline: Dollar Surges Against Yen, Euro With a Lift From U.S. Equities, *Wall Street Journal*, August 7, 2002

    Commentary: This was a great signal. The EURUSD had declined from 1.0127 on July 19th to .9621 on August 6th. The EURUSD

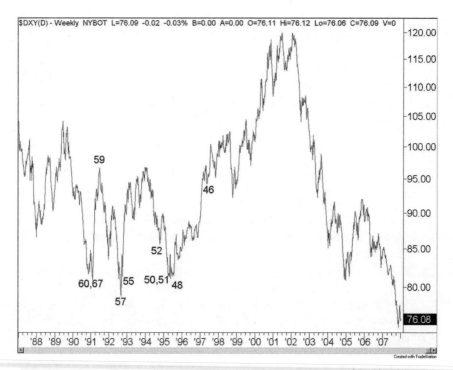

FIGURE 4.5 U.S. Dollar Index Weekly Bars with Articles Denoted By Numbers
Source: Chart created on TradeStation®, the flagship product of TradeStation Technologies, Inc.

exploded higher in the weeks and months that followed this headline.

17. Headline: Dollar Surges Against Yen, Gains Slightly on Euro, *Wall Street Journal*, April 10, 2001

    Commentary: This headline came after the USDJPY had topped at 126.86 on April 2nd. On the 10th, the pair closed at 124.43. Less than two months later, the USDJPY was testing 118.00.

18. Headline: Dollar Surges Against Yen, Improves On Euro Amid U.S. Yield Advantage, *Wall Street Journal*, May 20, 1999

    Commentary: It does not get any better than this one. After rallying from 108.22 to 124.90 in a four-month span, the USDJPY topped on May 19th at 124.90 and fell close to 101.00 by the end of November.

19. Headline: Dollar Surges on Signs the Japanese Are United in Seeking a Weaker Yen, *Wall Street Journal*, February 17, 1999

    Commentary: This headline appeared at the beginning of a larger topping process for the USDJPY.

20. Headline: Dollar Surges Against Yen and Mark As Stability Returns to World Markets, *Wall Street Journal*, November 10, 1998

Commentary: After rallying from 113.55 to 122.37 in less than a month, the USDJPY spiked to 124.12 on the 12th but then fell to 108.22 by January 11, 1999.

21. Headline: Currency Traders Fear Surge by Yen; Dollar Posts Advance Against the Mark, *Wall Street Journal*, October 20, 1998

Commentary: The USDJPY had fallen from 147 to 114 by October 20th. The pair rallied to 123.15 by the end of November.

22. Headline: Dollar Surges Against Mark But Plunges in Pound Trading, *New York Times*, July 3, 1997

Commentary: The GBPUSD had rallied from nearly 1.6000 to nearly 1.7000 when this headline was published. The pair closed at 1.6885 on the 3rd and ranged for a week before falling to 1.5775 by mid-August.

23. Headline: Pound's Surge and Comment By Japan's Chief Hurt Dollar, *New York Times*, June 24, 1997

Commentary: The USD Index was at 95.18 the day that this headline was published. The index rallied through 101.00 by August.

24. Headline: Dollar Tumbles Against the Mark, Yen As Strong GDP Data Spook Bond Market, *Wall Street Journal*, May 3, 1996

Commentary: The USDJPY has declined from 108.67 to 104.83 (on a closing basis) from April 12th to May 3rd. The pair rallied to 110.9 by early July.

25. Headline: Canadian Dollar Surges in Asia After Quebec Rejects Secession, *New York Times*, October 31, 1995

Commentary: This headline appeared on a day that would mark a low for the next year. The USDCAD rallied from 1.3400 to 1.3800 by January and would not reach 1.3400 again until the end of October 1996.

26. Headline: Dollar Plunges Further as the Selloff Continues, *Wall Street Journal*, September 22, 1995

Commentary: This was the beginning of the bottoming process for the U.S. dollar.

27. Headline: Dollar Surges on Japanese Intervention And Cut by Germany in Its Repo Rate, *Wall Street Journal*, September 7, 1995

Commentary: The dollar rallied significantly in August 1995. On September 7th, the USD Index stood at 86.12. A high was made on the 13th at 87.12, and the index fell to 83.00 by mid-October.

28. Headlines: Dollar Surges On New Plan To Cut Deficit, *New York Times*, May 12, 1995, and Dollar Surges Against Yen And Mark On

House Panel's Vote To Curb Deficit, *Wall Street Journal*, May 12, 1995

Commentary: Headlines detailing the surge in two newspapers. The Dollar Index had rallied from roughly 80 to 84 in a month. On May 13th, the index closed at 84.04. A high was made at 84.58 on the 23rd before the index fell back to 81 in just three days.

29. Headline: Dollar Falls Sharply in Japan, *New York Times*, April 17, 1995

   Commentary: The USDJPY made its all-time low the next day.

30. Headline: Dollar Surges With Financial Markets; Japan's Purchases, Weaker Mark Cited, *Wall Street Journal*, August 25, 1994

   Commentary: The USD Index fell from near 90 to below 85.00 in the days and weeks that followed the release of this headline.

31. Headline: Dollar Posts Surge Against The Mark On Speculation Fed Weighs Rate Boost, *Wall Street Journal*, February 4, 1994

   Commentary: Early February 1994 was a double top and significant multiyear high for the USD Index.

32. Headlines: The Buck Stops—Cold—as Yen Continues to Surge, *Los Angeles Times*, August 19, 1993, and Fed Action Drives Dollar's Surge Against Yen, *Wall Street Journal*, August 20, 1993

   Commentary: Another double headline. The USDJPY put in a nearly nine-month low on August 16th. The USDJPY rallied from 101 to 113 in the four and a half months that followed this headline.

33. Headline: Dollar's Surge Kills Yen's Rally, Rise Against Mark Is Expected To Weaken, *Wall Street Journal*, June 21, 1993

   Commentary: The day that this headline was published, the USDJPY stood at 111.05. The pair declined to 101 a little less than two months later.

34. Headline: Dollar Surges on Reduction By Germany of Interest Rate, *New York Times*, March 6, 1993

   Commentary: The 6th was a Saturday but the USD Index opened at 94.29 on the 8th. The index would reach a high of 94.53 on the 15th before falling to 88.50 by late April.

35. Headline: Dollar Surges against Mark, Sterling in Delayed Response to Oil-Price Jump, *Wall Street Journal*, May 28, 1992

   Commentary: From May 19th to May 28th, the USD Index rallied from 86.75 to 88.83 but then fell to 78.33 by September.

The "Dollar" and "Plunge" Search

36. Headline: Dollar Plunge Leads Supermodel to Demand Euros, *The New American*, November 26, 2007

Commentary: Published a few days following a high of 1.4967. The EURUSD fell to 1.4310 less than one month later.

37. Headline: Dollar Plunges On Snow Chill, But Stocks Rise; Treasury Chief Hints Bush Team Won't Act to Lift the Currency, *Wall Street Journal*, November 18, 2004

    Commentary: Granted, the EURUSD did continue to rally for another month following this release but from December 30th to November 15th, the EURUSD fell from 1.3666 to 1.1638.

38. Headline: Dollar Plunges Against Rivals As Bearish Outlook Growls Anew, *Wall Street Journal*, January 21, 2004

    Commentary: This article appeared in the middle of a EURUSD topping (U.S. dollar bottoming process). On the 21st, the EURUSD was at 1.2632. The pair fell over 300 pips by the end of January and was down nearly 1,000 pips by the end of April.

39. Headline: Dollar Plunges Against the Pound; Prospect of Rate Increases In U.K. Hits U.S. Currency As Other Rivals Also Gain, *Wall Street Journal*, October 23, 2003

    Commentary: This was a decent short-term signal. The GBPUSD closed at 1.6956 on the 23rd and made a high on the 29th at 1.7075 before falling over 500 pips in one week.

40. Headlines: Dollar Plunge Knocks US Status, *Euromoney*, London, June 2003, and Dollar Plunges Against Euro, Drawing Close to Record Low, *New York Times*, May 24, 2003

    Commentary: *Euromoney* is a monthly publication and the *New York Times* published a U.S. dollar bearish feature in late May. The EURUSD made a high on June 13th at 1.1930 and fell to 1.0765 by September before resuming its uptrend.

41. Headline: Pound Plunges Against Dollar Amid Focus on the U.K. Election, *Wall Street Journal*, June 7, 2001

    Commentary: One of the best contrarian signals I have seen with regard to *Wall Street Journal* headlines. The GBPUSD had declined steadily for months and in June 2001 (June 12th, to be exact), the GBPUSD formed a low at 1.3682. In October, the pair reached 1.4800.

42. Headline: Dollar Gains on Yen, Falls Against Euro After Common Currency Plunges in Asia, *Wall Street Journal*, June 6, 2001

    Commentary: The EURUSD was forming its secondary low at this time that led to the multiyear bull move.

43. Headline: Yen Plunges Against Dollar, *New York Times*, March 31, 2001

    Commentary: March 31st was a Saturday but the USDJPY opened at 126.16 on April 2nd and made a high that day that would not be seen for over eight months.

44. Headlines: Euro Continues Recent Plunge, Yet Officials Show No Alarm, *Wall Street Journal,* November 30, 1999, and Yen's Rise, Euro's Plunge Raise Concerns, *Wall Street Journal,* November 29, 1999

Commentary: The EURUSD had been falling steadily and closed at 1.0087 on November 30. The pair would trade no lower than .9991 on its way to 1.0415 by early January.

45. Headline: Yen's Plunge Takes Toll Around World, *Wall Street Journal,* June 16, 1998

Commentary: An amazing signal. The USDJPY topped out on the day of the headline at 146.78 and fell to 133.70 in three days. A secondary high was made in August before the JPY gained significantly (the USDJPY was nearly 100 a year and a half later).

46. Headline: Dollar Plunges As Fear Of Intervention Begins To Rise, *Wall Street Journal,* May 12, 1997

Commentary: The USD Index hit a low of 94.28 on the 12th and enjoyed a brief rally before falling to 93.07 on the 21st. The index then skyrocketed through 101 in August.

47. Headline: Sterling Plunges as Concern Emerges About Economic Impact of Recent Gains, *Wall Street Journal,* December 4, 1996

Commentary: The GBPUSD closed at 1.6387 on December 4th and at 1.6268 on December 5th before rallying through 1.7100 in less than a month.

48. Headline: Dollar Plunges As Investors Conclude New Interest-Rate Cut Isn't Very Likely, *Wall Street Journal,* July 20, 1995

Commentary: A significant bottom was formed around this time.

49. Headlines: Dollar Plunges Against The Yen; Japan Intervenes, *New York Times,* April 10, 1995; Dollar Plunges to a Record Low Of 83.71 Yen, Off 16% on Year, *New York Times,* April 8, 1995; and Dollar Tumbles Below 84 Yen And Traders See New Weakness, *New York Times,* April 7, 1995

Commentary: Three headlines dedicated to the USDJPY decline and the USDJPY made its all-time low on April 19th.

50. Headline: A Wild Day For The Markets As Dollar Resumes Its Plunge, *New York Times,* April 1, 1995

Commentary: Headline was published just two weeks before the multiyear low was formed on April 18th.

51. Headlines: Dollar Plunges Again, Setting Off Stock Selloff, *Los Angeles Times,* March 8, 1995; Dollar Continues To Plunge As U.S. Ponders Strategy, *New York Times,* March 7, 1995; and Dollar's Plunge And The Mark's Surge Continue, *Wall Street Journal,* March 7, 1995

Commentary: The USD Index hit 81.63 on March 7th and rallied 84.41 by March 10th. Notice how many headlines were about the U.S. dollar plunging in March and April of 1995, just before one of the largest rallies in U.S. dollar history began.

52. Headline: Dollar Plunges After Bentsen Says U.S. Doesn't Plan Intervention To Support It, *Wall Street Journal*, October 21, 1994

    Commentary: The 21st was a Friday and the USD Index closed that day at 85.63. It traded down to 84.91 on the next Tuesday and then tagged 90 on December 21st.

53. Headline: Dollar Takes Plunge As Germany's Kohl Is Thought To Disavow Interest Rate Cuts, *Wall Street Journal*, January 28, 1994

    Commentary: A decent short-term signal. The USD Index rallied from 95 to 97 in the week that followed this headline.

54. Headline: Sterling Plunges, Continuing To React To Lower U.K. Rates As Dollar Rises, *Wall Street Journal*, January 28, 1993

    Commentary: The GBPUSD made a multiyear low a few weeks after this headline on February 12th at 1.4180. Within three months, the pair was testing 1.6000.

55. Headline: Dollar Continues Its Plunge as Market Remains Bearish About U.S. Economy, *Wall Street Journal*, September 30, 1992

    Commentary: The USD Index made a secondary low on September 29th at 81.04 and the index was above 90 by the end of the year.

56. Headline: Dollar Soars Again; Dow Adds 11 Market Overview, *Los Angeles Times*, September 19, 1992

    Commentary: The 19th was a Saturday but a short-term top was put in place the next week at 84.52. The USD Index dropped to 81.04 by the end of the month.

57. Headline: Dollar's Plunge Sends Costs Skyrocketing for American Scholars Working Abroad, *The Chronicle of Higher Education*, September 9, 1992

    Headline: Down and Down the Dollar Goes, *Time*, September 7, 1992

    Headline: Dollar Plunge Leaves Stock Market Shaky, *Christian Science Monitor*, August 27, 1992

    Headline: Dollar's Plunge Worries U.S. and Europe, *Wall Street Journal*, August 25, 1992

    Headline: Dollar, in Plunge, Hits All-Time Low against the Mark, *New York Times*, August 22, 1992

    Commentary: Dollar doomsday articles were appearing in nearly every publication in late August and early September 1992. Of course, the USD Index made a low in September 1992 that would not be approached for 25 years.

58. Headline: Dollar Plunges after Federal Reserve Signals It's Seeking Lower Interest Rates, *Wall Street Journal*, April 10, 1992

    Commentary: This signal was good for a rally from 88.50 to 90.50 in the USD Index within a one-week span.

59. Headline: The Dominant Dollar; Highflying Greenback a Windfall for Foreign Firms, but Could Deflate Export Boom, *The Washington Post*, July 14, 1991

    Commentary: The dominance ended three days before this article was published. The USD Index steadily declined from July 1991 until January 1992.

60. Headline: Watching the Dollar Tumble, *Christian Science Monitor*, November 8, 1990

    Headline: How Dollar's Plunge Aids Some Companies, Does Little for Others, *Wall Street Journal*, October 22, 1990

    Headline: Dollar's Plunge May Keep Rates Up, Economists Warn, *Los Angeles Times*, October 20, 1990

    Headline: Dollar Plunges against Yen; Gold Prices Move Higher, *New York Times*, October 18, 1990

    Commentary: These headlines appear at the beginning of a rally from just above 80 to just below 100 in the USD Index.

61. Headline: U.S. Unit Plunges to a 28-Month Low against Mark on Interest-Rate Jitters, *Wall Street Journal*, May 10, 1990

    Commentary: On May 10th, the USD Index closed at 91.21. One month later, the index had rallied through 93.

62. Headline: Dollar Soars Against the Yen; Stocks Drop, *The Washington Post*, March 28, 1990

    Commentary: The USDJPY was at a multiyear high near 160 when this headline hit newswires. On the 28th, the USDJPY was at 158.75. A high was made at 159.90 on April 17th and the USDJPY began its decline to 81.12.

63. Headline: Dollar Plunges As Bundesbank Surprises Market, *Wall Street Journal*, January 5, 1990

    Commentary: This signal was good for a rally from 92.50 to 94.30 over a three-week period.

The "Dollar" and "Plummet" Search

64. Headline: Euro Continues to Plummet Against Dollar, Yen, *Wall Street Journal*, September 20, 2000

Commentary: On September 20th, the EURUSD closed at .8439. The pair would rally to .8850 by the end of the month and then make its final low at .8247 in October.

65. Headline: Dollar Plummets, Yen Soars on New Japan Optimism, *Los Angeles Times*, October 8, 1998

Commentary: The USDJPY made a short-term low in the week that followed this headline and rallied over 800 pips by the end of November.

66. Headline: Dollar Plummets 2.8%, As 3M Pierces Stocks, *Wall Street Journal*, December 18, 1997

Commentary: The USD Index rallied from 98.50 to 101.50 in the two weeks that followed this headline.

67. Headline: Dollar Plummets Despite Intervention; U.S. Says It Isn't Seeking Depreciation, *Wall Street Journal*, February 7, 1991

Commentary: The USD Index made a significant low on February 7th at 80.49. By July the index was above 97.

68. Headline: Tokyo Stock Prices Plummet, Dollar Surges Against the Yen, *Los Angeles Times*, April 10, 1990

Commentary: The USDJPY closed April 10th at 158.58, rallied to 159.90 by July 17th and then fell to 125.05 in six months.

Below are a few headlines that I have come across that predict an outcome or take a strong directional stance. These are typically the most reliable contrarian signals because sentiment must be as extreme as it is going to get for a financial reporter to feel confident enough to put forth a forecast in the headline.

Media Prognostications

69. Headline: Dollar Is Expected to Stay Weak Against Euro, Yen, *Wall Street Journal*, November 26, 2007

Headline: Put Your Hands in the Air . . . For the Euro, That Is; From Jay-Z to Warren-B, Euro Is Gaining Currency, *Wall Street Journal*, November 19, 2007

Commentary: The EURUSD fell the most in four years from November 23rd to December 20th.

70. Headline: U.S. Trade Deficit Isn't Likely to Devastate Dollar, *Wall Street Journal*, June 18, 2004

Commentary: One month after this headline, the EURUSD had rallied over 500 pips. By the end of 2004, the EURUSD had rallied over 1,600 pips from the June 18th close.

71. Headline: Dollar Is Expected to Remain Strong On Optimism Over Economy and War, *Wall Street Journal*, November 19, 2001

Commentary: Just four days later, on November 23rd, the EURUSD made a low that is still in place at .8372. The pair rallied to .9500 in just over a month's time.

72. Headline: At Last, the Euro Looks Ready to Climb, *New York Times*, July 25, 1999

    Commentary: It was not quite time for the EURUSD to rally. The pair closed at 1.0645 on the 26th (the 25th was a Sunday) and steadily declined until reaching its all-time low at .8227 in October 2000.

73. Headline: Canadian Dollar Appears Attractive Amid Uncertainties In Other Countries, *Wall Street Journal*, March 22, 1993

    Commentary: This headline appeared during a week that saw the USDCAD make a multiyear low (Canadian dollar high).

WHERE TO LOOK

The easiest way to search for headlines is to go to finance.google.com. On the right side of the web page, you will see prices for USD-Euro, USD-JPY, and USD-GBP. Click on any rate. If you click on USD-Euro, you will come to a page that features a chart along with U.S. dollar articles. On the right side of the page, click on View all news for USDEUR. It does not matter what the second currency is in the pair, the news headlines returned are always for the first currency in the pair (in this case, USD for USDEUR). The most read articles will appear first. Simply scan the headlines. You can also view a chart for news volume on the right side of this page. Spikes in volume will occur at major turning points.

If you have a subscription to the Wall Street Journal Online, you can actually do a search for all news sources that are owned by Dow Jones. Clicking on advanced search at the top of wsj.com will bring up the Search Resource Center. Click on advanced search options. Select headline within the dropdown box "Search for terms in." Type the currency name in the search and click on search. This bit of research takes 5 to 10 minutes a day at most and will prove most rewarding.

Most of the time, the headlines contain what I consider ordinary language such as "Dollar Rallies against Euro." This would signal that the probability of a reversal is low so the best strategy is to remain with the trend.

CONCLUSION

As you can see from the examples in this chapter, headlines that contain strong language and/or that take a directional stand are fantastic contrarian signals. How you use this information is up to you, of course. You might use the actual headline as an exit strategy and wait for a higher probability entry (see "Determining a Bias" in Chapter 6). Or, if a headline occurs when other information indicates that a change in trend is a high probability (COT, consecutive periods in one direction, and so forth), then acting on the signal is probably warranted. In any case, understand that this is a risky trade outright. These headlines appear after a sharp move in price when conditions are volatile. Also, if the market is at a multiweek/month/year high or low, then there is no simple answer to the question "Where do I place my stop?" unless of course you are familiar with the wave principle (see Chapter 7). Additional timing tools such as pivot points can also be used.

CHAPTER 5

Sentiment
Indicators

T he charts in Chapter 2 of various economic indicators plotted with the USD Index (DXY) show that there is absolutely no relationship between any one economic indicator and the U.S. dollar.

Critics will argue that you cannot use just one economic indicator. They will say that you have to look at a number of indicators and understand the big picture. The problem with this approach is that most economic indicators are positively correlated; they move together (go back to Chapter 2 and take a look at those indicators again). So even though accurately forecasting one economic number with another economic number might be possible, accurately forecasting the direction of a currency with an economic number is not possible.

Others will argue that economic numbers do play a role but that a host of other variables are also important, such as war, the price of commodities (oil or gold, for example), and Black Swan events as described by Nassim Taleb in *The Black Swan: The Impact of the Highly Improbable*.[1] According to Taleb, a Black Swan is an unpredictable event that has an enormous impact on society, such as the September 11, 2001, terrorist attacks or the success of Google. Many traders believe that a combination of different variables is responsible for market movements, and I think this is closer to the truth. It is not the news of war, the price of oil, the release of an economic indicator, or even a Black Swan event that causes market trends, but rather the collective response of all market participants to all of these events. The end result is that the market moves, and the only reason for that movement is this: The market (all market participants) responded a certain way (bullish or bearish) because psychology is this or that (bullish or bearish). That is it. The market has a mind of its own. Understanding this point will save you from wondering why a market moved down on supposedly bullish news and up on supposedly bearish news. The only way to consistently trade on the correct side of the market is to understand the psychological state of that market. In other words, what is the sentiment?

Chapter 4 provided a list of actual headlines, most taken from respected financial periodicals. The mainstream financial media attempts to report the reasons for market movements to the public. Think for a second, and you will realize how futile that exercise is. As mentioned, there are many different variables that traders respond to, and ultimately the collective psychology wins out. Did the reporter ask every single person who was trading the EURUSD that day why he or she bought or sold? No, the reporter is instead fitting news to the price action.

The simple explanation that market psychology is the reason for a bull or bear move does not satisfy the public. As such, an entire industry has been created to literally come up with reasons why. At the end of the day the ultimate reason that the market moves one way or the other is psychological; therefore, the study of sentiment indicators is paramount to determining the highest probability move.

In this chapter, I present different sentiment indicators and how to use them in order to spot market turns. Most of the chapter focuses on the Commitments of Traders (COT) reports. I will take you through the process of how I construct indicators with the COT data. I find the COT data very useful, and the information is free to download at www.cftc.gov. Besides, trading is a business, and you should try and keep your costs to a minimum.

COMMITMENTS OF TRADERS REPORTS

The COT reports are, in my opinion, one of the most useful yet neglected sources of information for traders. The reports detail the positioning of speculative and commercial traders in the various futures markets. In spot FX, there are no volume indicators to analyze because trades do not pass through a centralized exchange (the FX market is an over-the-counter market, or OTC); therefore, we must rely on COT data from the futures market, which we can use as a proxy for the spot market. These figures can be analyzed to gauge the psychological state of a market.

The reports are released weekly via the Commodity Futures Trading Commission (CFTC) and, as mentioned, can be downloaded for free at www.cftc.gov.

HISTORY OF U.S. FUTURES TRADING

Futures trading has an extensive and interesting history. The modern history begins in Chicago in the 1840s. Chicago was a natural center for transportation, distribution, and trading of agricultural produce because the city is close to the Midwestern United States, where a great deal of the country's farmland is located. Shortages of agricultural produce led to violent fluctuations in price which posed the risk of adverse price change to merchants. The development of a market that enabled grain merchants and agriculture companies to trade in futures contracts was a way for these entities to hedge risk. In 1848, the Chicago Board of Trade (CBOT) was formed as the world's first futures exchange. The Chicago Produce Exchange was formed in 1874 and was renamed the Chicago Mercantile Exchange (CME) in 1898 (currency futures trade on the CME). As mentioned, the CFTC regulates futures trading in the United States but the commission was not formed until 1974. Here are some important dates from the web site www.cftc.gov regarding the history of futures trading before the creation of the CFTC.

1880s: The first bills are introduced in Congress to regulate, ban, or tax futures trading in the U.S. Over the next 40 years, approximately 200 such bills will be introduced.

June 15, 1936: The Commodity Exchange Act is enacted. The Commodity Exchange Act replaces the Grain Futures Act and extends Federal regulation to a list of enumerated commodities that includes cotton, rice, mill feeds, butter, eggs, and Irish potatoes, as well as the grains. All references to "grains" in the Grain Futures Act are changed to "commodities." The Grain Futures Commission becomes the Commodity Exchange Commission and continues to consist of the Secretary of Agriculture, the Secretary of Commerce, and the Attorney General. The Commodity Exchange Act grants the Commodity Exchange Commission the authority to establish Federal speculative position limits, but not the authority to require exchanges to set their own speculative position limits. The Commodity Exchange Act, among other things, also requires futures commission merchants to segregate customer funds that are deposited for purposes of margin, prohibits fictitious and fraudulent transactions such as wash sales and accommodation trades, and bans all commodity option trading. The option ban remains in effect until 1981.

July 1, 1936: The Commodity Exchange Administration is formed within the USDA to succeed the Grain Futures Administration and administer the Commodity Exchange Act.

April 7, 1938: The Commodity Exchange Act is amended to add wool tops (a type of processed wool that is ready to be manufactured into textiles) to the list of regulated commodities.

December 22, 1938: The Commodity Exchange Commission promulgates the first Federal speculative position limits for futures contracts in grains (then defined as wheat, corn, oats, barley, flaxseed, grain sorghums, and rye), following an extended public comment period and hearings on the record.

August 26, 1940: The Commodity Exchange Commission establishes a Federal speculative position limit for cotton futures contracts.

October 9, 1940: The Commodity Exchange Act is amended to add fats and oils (including lard, tallow, cottonseed oil, peanut oil, soybean oil, and all other fats and oils), cottonseed meal, cottonseed, peanuts, soybeans, and soybean meal to the list of regulated commodities.

February 23, 1942: The Commodity Exchange Administration is merged with other agencies to form the Agricultural Marketing Administration. The organization is now known as the Commodity Exchange Branch of the Agricultural Marketing Administration.

December 19, 1947: The Commodity Exchange Act is amended to enable the Secretary of Agriculture to submit to Congress (pursuant to a congressional subpoena issued two days earlier) and make public the names, addresses, and market positions of large traders (which the Commodity Exchange Act normally requires be kept confidential). Shortly thereafter, the Secretary submits and publishes 35,000 large trader reports.

February 19, 1968: In the first major commodities legislation since 1936, the Commodity Exchange Act is amended to, among other things, add livestock and livestock products (e.g., live cattle, pork bellies) to the list of regulated commodities and institute minimum net financial requirements for futures commission merchants. The 1968 amendments also enhanced the enforcement provisions of the Act in various ways, including enhanced reporting requirements, increases in criminal penalties for manipulation and other violations of the Act, and a provision allowing for the suspension of contract market designation of any board of trade that fails to enforce its own rules.

1973: Grain and soybean futures prices reach record highs. This is blamed in part on excessive speculation and there are allegations of manipulation. Congress begins to consider revising the Federal regulatory scheme for commodities.

October 23–24, 1974: Congress passes the Commodity Futures Trading Commission Act of 1974, and it is signed by President Gerald Ford. The bill overhauls the Commodity Exchange Act and creates the

Commodity Futures Trading Commission (CFTC or Commission), an independent agency with powers greater than those of its predecessor agency, the Commodity Exchange Authority. For example, while the Commodity Exchange Authority only regulated agricultural commodities enumerated in the Commodity Exchange Act, the 1974 act granted the CFTC exclusive jurisdiction over futures trading in all commodities.

CURRENCY FUTURES HISTORY

Following the collapse of Bretton Woods, a group of commodity traders at the Chicago Mercantile Exchange (CME) naturally wanted to take advantage of free floating currencies by trading in them. Unfortunately for them, they did not have access to the inter-bank market. Refusing to give up and possibly miss big profits by not trading in the new arena, the group of traders established the International Monetary Market (IMM), which is now a division of the CME. On May 16, 1972, seven currency futures contracts began trading as the first financial futures. Previously limited to large commercial banks and their corporate customers, now individuals, investment funds, governments, and just about anyone else could buy and sell currencies for future delivery or cash settlement. Of course, anyone who opens a forex trading account with a forex dealer member has access to the spot market today. Tighter spreads, 24-hour trading, and customizable leverage are just some of the benefits that the forex market enjoys over currency futures.

ABOUT THE COT (abstracted from www.cftc.gov)
The Commitments of Traders (COT) reports can be traced back to 1924. In that year, the U.S. Department of Agriculture's Grain Futures Administration (predecessor to the USDA Commodity Exchange Authority, in turn the predecessor to the CFTC), published its first comprehensive annual report of hedging and speculation in regulated futures markets.

Beginning as of June 30, 1962, COT data were published each month. Those original reports then were compiled on an end-of-month basis and published on the 11th or 12th calendar day of the following month.

Over the years, the CFTC has improved the Commitments of Traders reports in several ways as part of its continuing effort to better inform the public about futures markets.

- *The COT report is published more often—switching to mid-month and month-end in 1990, to every two weeks in 1992, and weekly in 2000.*

- *The COT report is released more quickly—moving the publication to the sixth business day after the "as of" date in 1990 and then to the third business day after the "as of" date in 1992.*
- *The report also is more widely available—moving from a subscription-based mailing list to fee-based electronic access in 1993, and, beginning in 1995, becoming freely available on www.cftc.gov.*

The COT reports provide a breakdown of each Tuesday's open interest for markets in which 20 or more traders hold positions equal to or above the reporting levels established by the CFTC. The reports are released every Friday at 3:30 P.M. Eastern time.

Reports are available in both a short and long format. The short report shows open interest separately by reportable and non-reportable positions.

Current and historical Commitments of Traders data is available on www.cftc.gov, as is historical COT data going back to 1986 for Futures-Only reports

READING THE COT REPORT

The short report is sufficient for our purposes since all we need to know is net speculative positioning, net commercial positioning, and open interest (see Figure 5.1).

```
CANADIAN DOLLAR - CHICAGO MERCANTILE EXCHANGE                    Code-090741
FUTURES ONLY POSITIONS AS OF 12/31/07                       |
------------------------------------------------------------| NONREPORTABLE
     NON-COMMERCIAL     |    COMMERCIAL   |     TOTAL      |   POSITIONS
----------------------- |-----------------|----------------|-----------------
 LONG | SHORT |SPREADS |  LONG  | SHORT   | LONG  | SHORT  |  LONG  | SHORT

(CONTRACTS OF CAD 100,000)                       OPEN INTEREST:      83,024
COMMITMENTS
 35,655   12,657    1,405   18,604   52,488   55,664   66,550   27,360   16,474

CHANGES FROM 12/24/07 (CHANGE IN OPEN INTEREST:       5,667)
  5,696   -2,579      0    -309    7,048    5,387    4,469       280    1,198

PERCENT OF OPEN INTEREST FOR EACH CATEGORY OF TRADERS
  42.9     15.2      1.7    22.4     63.2     67.0     80.2      33.0     19.8

NUMBER OF TRADERS IN EACH CATEGORY (TOTAL TRADERS:        65)
    25       10        5     18       19       47       30
```

FIGURE 5.1 A short report for Canadian dollar futures shows the critical information: non-commercial and commercial positioning and open interest
Source: Courtesy of the U.S. Commodity Futures Trading Commission (www.cftc.gov).

It is important to familiarize yourself with the details of the report so you know what you're looking at. The COT reports contain much more information than just open interest and commercial and non-commercial positioning, but these three numbers are the meat of the report and are what I analyze. You can find more details at www.cftc.gov, such as the definitions below.

Open Interest
Open interest is the total of all futures and/or option contracts entered into and not yet offset by a transaction, by delivery, by exercise, etc. The aggregate of all long open interest is equal to the aggregate of all short open interest.

Commercial and Non-Commercial Traders
When an individual reportable trader is identified to the Commission, the trader is classified either as "commercial" or "non-commercial." All of a trader's reported futures positions in a commodity are classified as commercial if the trader uses futures contracts in that particular commodity for hedging. To ensure that traders are classified with accuracy and consistency, Commission staff may exercise judgment in re-classifying a trader if it has additional information about the trader's use of the markets.

A trader may be classified as a commercial trader in some commodities and as a non-commercial trader in other commodities. A single trading entity cannot be classified as both a commercial and non-commercial trader in the same commodity. Nonetheless, a multi-functional organization that has more than one trading entity may have each trading entity classified separately in a commodity. For example, a financial organization trading in financial futures may have a banking entity whose positions are classified as commercial and have a separate money-management entity whose positions are classified as non-commercial.

USING COT DATA WITH SPOT FX PRICE CHARTS

All spot FX trades are conducted on a relative basis. For example, if you are long the EURUSD, then your bet is that the euro will appreciate relative to the U.S. dollar. Similarly, if you are short the USDJPY, then your bet is that the dollar will fall relative to the Japanese yen or that the Japanese yen will appreciate relative to the dollar. The first currency in the pair is referred to as the base currency, and the second currency in the pair is referred to as the counter currency.

For example, the dollar is the base currency in USDJPY and the Japanese yen is the counter currency. COT data shows positioning details on the currency future itself, such as the euro or the Japanese yen. An extreme bullish reading on JPY warns of a top in JPY, which correlates to a bottom in the USDJPY. When the U.S. dollar is the base currency (USDJPY, USDCHF, USDCAD), keep this specific detail in mind.

UNDERSTANDING THE DATA

The CFTC's web site states that "The COT reports provide a breakdown of each Tuesday's open interest for markets in which 20 or more traders hold positions equal to or above the reporting levels established by the CFTC." Who wouldn't want to know this information? Remember that market tops and bottoms are created by the errors of optimism and pessimism that are referred to so often in this book. The COT report gives us actual numbers so that we can quantify where the market is in the constant oscillation between optimism and pessimism and, as a result, gain a big-picture understanding of a specific market.

As mentioned, there are two main groups that report positions: non-commercials (speculators) and commercials (hedgers). The non-commercial group consists primarily of large individual traders and hedge funds. The commercial group refers mostly to farmers (producers) for agricultural commodities and banks or multinational corporations for financial futures such as currencies.

For example, Toyota's headquarters are based in Japan, but the company manufactures a lot of cars in the United States. Toyota needs to exchange Japanese yen for U.S. dollars in order to pay U.S. employees in dollars. An entire new risk to the bottom line—currency risk—enters the equation now for Toyota. If the U.S. dollar appreciates significantly against the Japanese yen (USD/JPY increases), then Toyota takes a hit to its bottom line due to the increased cost incurred by paying U.S. employees in a more expensive currency. To guard against this risk, the treasurer of Toyota will buy U.S. dollar futures on the New York Board of Trade (NYBOT) and/or sell Japanese yen futures on the CME. Now, a price for U.S. dollars is basically locked in, and Toyota can concentrate on making cars instead of worrying about currency risk.

WATCHING THE COMMERCIALS

Larry Williams, an expert on the COT reports, was the first (at least to my knowledge) to recognize the importance of aligning with the commercials at market extremes. In *Trade Stocks and Commodities with the Insiders: Secrets of the COT Report,* Williams details his observations and explains that the commercials are always the longest (most bullish) at market bottoms and the shortest (most bearish) at market tops (see Figures 5.2 to 5.4). Very long at market bottoms and very short at market tops. Now that sounds like an excellent trading strategy!

Remember, commercial traders in the currency arena such as banks and multinational corporations are hedgers and have enormously deep pockets. With each tick higher in price, the hedger is selling in order to hedge against a decline in price. The more price increases, the more the hedger sells in order to obtain a higher average sell price. The result of

FIGURE 5.2 Commercial traders were extremely short British pounds at market tops in October 1999, March 2005, and July 2007, and extremely long the currency at the major market bottom in December 2005

Source: Chart created on TradeStation®, the flagship product of TradeStation Technologies, Inc.

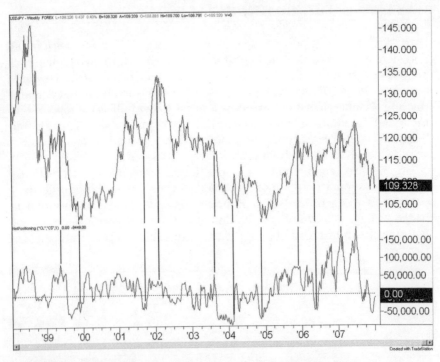

FIGURE 5.3 Commercial traders are extremely long JPY at market bottoms
(USDJPY tops) and extremely short JPY at market tops (USDJPY bottoms)
Source: Chart created on TradeStation®, the flagship product of TradeStation Technologies, Inc.

averaging down (selling and/or buying more contracts as price goes against
your position) is that the commercial trader is most bearish at the highest
price. Once price stops rising and begins to decline, the commercial trader
begins to buy futures in order to hedge against a rise in price. The same
process of averaging down occurs again, but this time the trader is buying as price is falling. The cycle of buying during downtrends and selling
during uptrends is continuous and results in owning the most at the bottom and the least at the top. The hedger is not trying to make a profit from
speculating on the price of the currency but is instead ensuring that price
movements in the currency do not adversely affect the profitability of the
core business, whether that is selling cars, clothes, or whatever.

WATCHING THE SPECULATORS

The hedge funds and individual traders that trade in a large enough
amount are required to report their positions to the CFTC. These are the

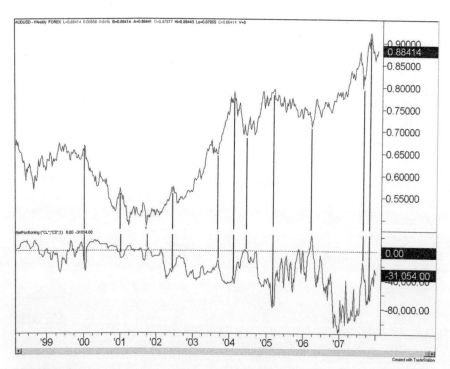

FIGURE 5.4 The same can be said for commercials and the Australian dollar. Peaks in buying occur at market bottoms and peaks in selling occur at market tops
Source: Chart created on TradeStation®, the flagship product of TradeStation Technologies, Inc.

non-commercial traders or, simply, the speculators. Generally speaking, speculators are trend followers. In other words, these traders buy as price increases and sell as price decreases. Figures 5.5 to 5.7 clearly show that trends in price and speculative positioning move together. Tops and bottoms in price and positioning tend to occur at the exact same time (often the same week). There are instances when the tops and/or bottoms in price and positioning occur a few weeks apart, but having the ability to identify a major market top or bottom within a two- or three-week window is obviously beneficial.

The errors of optimism and pessimism that Pigou referenced (refer back to Chapter 1 for the full quote) are clearly displayed in the charts above. An uptrend is established and speculators add to long positions, creating what can be described as a bullish sentiment extreme (error of optimism) until the market reverses. Traders then sell as price falls, which eventually leads to a bearish sentiment extreme (error of pessimism). This explanation of how markets work is overly simplistic and makes

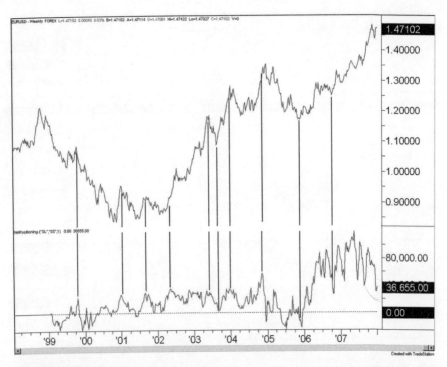

FIGURE 5.5 Speculators (non-commercial) are always wrong at market turns. Notice how speculative longs reach a peak as the EURUSD reaches a peak and a trough as the EURUSD reaches a trough
Source: Chart created on TradeStation®, the flagship product of TradeStation Technologies, Inc.

successful trading—buying low and selling high—seem exceptionally easy. However, if you can accept that sentiment is the true fundamental reason why prices trend and reverse, then you have an edge on your competitors (other traders). Understanding what actually affects market movements and what is just temporary noise is of utmost importance.

COMMERCIAL AND SPECULATORS GIVE THE SAME SIGNAL

You have probably noticed that speculative positioning and commercial positioning move inversely to one another. If a statement is made about the relationship between speculative positioning and price, then the opposite is true about commercial positioning and price. For example:

FIGURE 5.6 The tops and bottoms that were signaled in the GBPUSD by the commercial positioning are also signaled by the non-commercial positioning...except non-commercial traders are on the wrong side of the market at the turn
Source: Chart created on TradeStation®, the flagship product of TradeStation Technologies, Inc.

- Speculators are extremely long when commercials are extremely short (and vice versa).
- A top in price occurs when speculators are extremely long and when commercials are extremely short (and vice versa).
- Speculative positioning is on the correct side of the market for the meat of the move but is wrong at the turn.
- Commercial positioning is on the wrong side of the market for the meat of the move but is correct at the turn.

The last two points, while obvious, are extremely important. It is profitable to remain with the speculators (long or short) *until* a sentiment extreme has been reached. Once a sentiment extreme is registered, the risk of a reversal outweighs the potential reward that comes from the continuation of the trend. A sentiment extreme warns that the trend is close to an

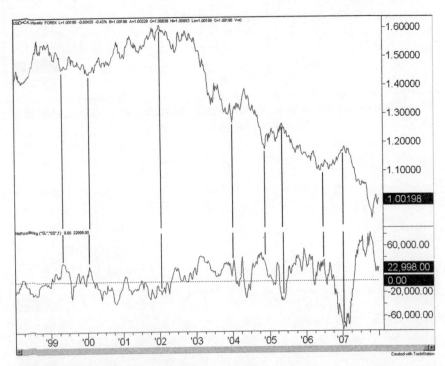

FIGURE 5.7 The dynamic is the same with the USDCAD. Speculators are extremely long Canadian dollars at CAD tops (USDCAD bottoms) and extremely short Canadian dollars at CAD bottoms (USDCAD tops)
Source: Chart created on TradeStation®, the flagship product of TradeStation Technologies, Inc.

end and that at least a period of consolidation will occur, and perhaps an outright reversal. With this in mind, the most important trading decisions are made as soon as a sentiment extreme is identified. More importantly, a sentiment extreme determines when to make a decision.

Sometimes (probably a lot more than sometimes), the best decision is to do nothing. For example, if you are long and there is no indication of a sentiment extreme, then remain long. You will probably hear hundreds of reasons why you should exit the trade, some fundamental and some technical. "There is event risk tomorrow" is a popular one as is "The pair is overbought." Ignore all of the noise and understand that market psychology (sentiment) remains bullish until an extreme is registered. In *Reminiscences of a Stock Operator*, the main character, Larry Livingston, best explains the virtue of patience and trading for the big move when he mentions that "It never was my thinking that made the big money for me. It always was my sitting."[2]

Every market top is accompanied by a sentiment extreme, but not every sentiment extreme leads to a market top. Market extremes, as we are defining them here, can last for weeks. This dynamic was described by John Maynard Keynes when he said that "The market can stay irrational longer than you can stay solvent." Still, exiting a few weeks early is better than exiting after a reversal because reversals, especially in a market as highly leveraged as the FX market, happen fast. So sit with the position until a sentiment extreme is registered; then make a decision.

There are of course other technical tools (see Chapter 6) that can and should be used at this point to aid in making the decision, but the point is that now you know when a decision needs to be made. For now, I would like to more concretely define *sentiment extreme* in terms of an indicator so that we can more objectively determine when a market is at an extreme and just as importantly, when a market is not at an extreme.

THE APPROACH

Studying commercial and speculative positioning as has been presented so far helps in determining when a market is at a potential turning point. However, taking a closer look at the data yields better results. Most of the rest of this chapter is dedicated to how I approach COT analysis and, more specifically, how I conclude whether or not a market is at a bullish or bearish extreme.

Combining the Speculators and Commercials

Every single peak in speculative positioning occurs at the exact same time as a trough in commercial positioning and vice versa (see Figure 5.8). Visually, it is obvious that a market turn occurs when the two groups significantly diverge from one another. What else is obvious? Commercial positioning moves inversely with price action, and speculative positioning moves with price action. With this understanding, it makes sense to combine the two groups and construct one composite COT.

Combining the groups into one indicator also makes for a cleaner chart. It is important to clearly see the price chart and keep technical indicators to a minimum. When looking at COT data, the charts used are weekly bars, and it is important that former significant highs and lows are clear so that support and resistance levels as well as breakouts are apparent. With three or four indicators on a chart, the price action is compressed and becomes difficult to view, especially when dealing with a small computer screen. After all, price is being traded, not the indicators. (Based on the amount of attention given to indicators, many traders seem to forget this fact.)

Further, I think it is more intuitive when the indicator moves with price action. A top in the indicator signaling a top in price makes more sense to me than a bottom in the indicator signaling a top in price. (Having said that, remember that the chart is flipped when the U.S. dollar is the base currency in the pair.) In order to ensure that the newly constructed index correlates positively with price action, the directionality of the indicator must be determined by the speculative positioning. Also, a market is defined as extreme when the two groups (commercial and speculative) diverge significantly. Subtracting commercial positioning from speculative positioning satisfies both requirements: The composite COT correlates positively with price, and the peaks (and troughs) of the indicator indicate when the two groups are most divergent with respect to positioning.

Composite COT = net speculative positioning − net commercial positioning

Constructing an Index

As the examples in Figures 5.9 to 5.10 illustrate, the composite COT is itself a valuable tool. However, determining whether or not a sentiment extreme exists in real time is too difficult a task with just the composite COT. Upper and lower boundaries would help in more objectively defining when a market is extreme, much like overbought and oversold in the Relative Strength Index (RSI) or a stochastics indicator. An easy way to create boundaries is by assigning a ranking between 0 and 100 for each value in our data set over a specified period of time. In other words, use percentiles to create an index. You can do this easily with the percentrank() function in Microsoft Excel.

If you're unfamiliar with the concept of percentiles, here are a few examples. Percentiles are used in the reporting of scores for standardized tests and for reporting height and weight. For example, if Joe's test score is better than 75 percent of all other test scores, then Joe's test score is at the 75th percentile. Similarly, a newborn boy who weighs 7 pounds, 11 ounces and is 21 inches long is at the 57th percentile in weight and at the 89th percentile in height. This means that the baby boy weighs the same or more than 57 percent of the reference population of baby boys and is as long or longer than 89 percent of the reference population of baby boys.

When determining whether a market is at a point where the probability of a reversal is greater than the probability of the trend continuing (extreme or not extreme), all that matters is the 0 percentile and the 100th percentile. A rank of 100 indicates that the difference between speculative

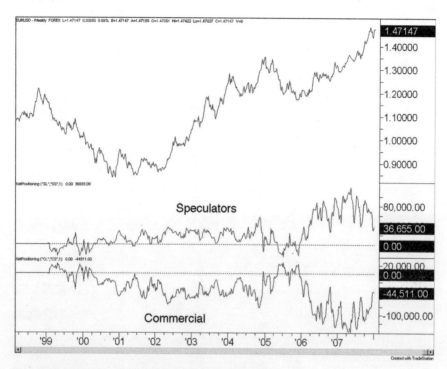

FIGURE 5.8 In this EURUSD chart with both speculative and commercial position-ing, it is clear that the two groups mirror each other
Source: Chart created on TradeStation®, the flagship product of TradeStation Tech-nologies, Inc.

and commercial positioning is the greatest or equal to the greatest differ-ence in our data set and that speculators are extremely long and commer-cials extremely short. An index reading of 100 signifies a bullish sentiment extreme. A rank of 0 indicates that the difference between speculative and commercial positioning is the greatest or equal to the greatest difference in our data set and that speculators are extremely short and commercials ex-tremely long. An index reading of 0 signifies a bearish sentiment extreme. The COT percentile indicator is referred to as the COT Index.

As mentioned, the COT reports are released every week (on Friday). In order to determine if a certain market is at a bullish or bearish senti-ment extreme, we have to specify how many weeks to include in the study. In other words, we must decide on the input length, much like deciding on a moving average length. As is the case with any technical indicator, a shorter input length will provide more but less reliable signals. A longer input length will provide fewer but more reliable signals. Fifty-two weeks

FIGURE 5.9 The Composite COT line combines the two groups. The line moves in tandem with price. Peaks in the Composite COT line correspond to peaks in the euro and vice versa
Source: Chart created on TradeStation®, the flagship product of TradeStation Technologies, Inc.

(one year) is an obvious input to begin with (try 26 and 13 for shorter-term signals).

A reading of 100 conveys that the composite COT is the highest it has been in 52 weeks (speculators extremely long and commercials extremely short). A reading of 0 conveys that the composite COT is the lowest it has been in 52 weeks (speculators extremely short and commercials extremely long). By using percentiles, the decision as to whether or not a market has reached a sentiment extreme is more objective. However, notice that the extreme signal can last for quite some time, as evidenced in Figure 5.11 (DXY). The COT Index reaches 0 in early October 2004. By blindly following the COT Index, you would have concluded that a bearish sentiment extreme was registered and that it was therefore time to begin buying dollars. As the chart shows, this would have been a very poor long entry since the dollar decline continued into December 2004. Also, the COT Index reaches

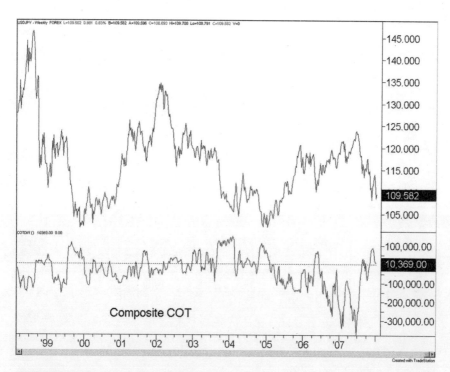

FIGURE 5.10 Remember that when the USD is the base currency, tops in the pair occur when the Composite COT line is at a trough and bottoms in the pair occur when the Composite COT line is at a peak
Source: Chart created on TradeStation®, the flagship product of TradeStation Technologies, Inc.

100 in May 2005. By blindly following this information, you would have concluded that a bullish extreme had been registered and that it was time to go against the crowd and begin selling dollars. Again, this plan would have either resulted in a margin call or a lot of pain since the rally continued into July of that year. The readings of 100 and 0 are too frequent and not timely enough to have confidence in. The problem is fixed once we take a closer look at the data.

Ratios

Proclaiming that a market has reached a bullish or bearish sentiment extreme based solely on *absolute* positioning is problematic. The general idea is good, but it does not make sense to look at only absolute positioning. For example, speculators were net long 38,786 contracts in December 2004 and

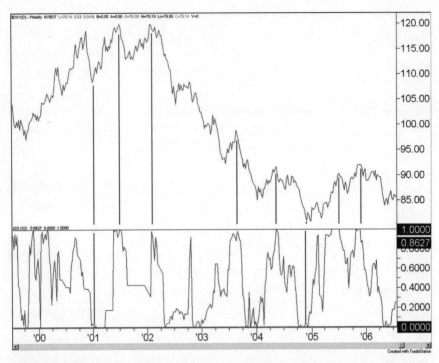

FIGURE 5.11 By filtering the Composite COT with a percentile (COT Index), signals are provided more objectively. Tops occur when the COT Index is at 100 and bottoms occur when the COT index is at 0
Source: Chart created on TradeStation®, the flagship product of TradeStation Technologies, Inc.

long 59,864 contracts in November 2006. From this information, we would conclude that there was a higher probability of a top occurring in November 2006 than in December 2004 because speculators were more bullish in November 2006...or were they? A closer look at the COT data is essential to properly understanding a market's psychological state. In December 2004, the breakdown for speculators was 41,235 long contracts and 2,449 short contracts for a net long total of 38,786. Of all speculative positions, 94 percent ($41,235 \div [41,235 + 2,449]$) were long positions. In November 2006, the breakdown for speculators was 80,509 long contracts and 20,645 short contracts for a net long total of 59,864. Eighty percent ($80,509 \div [80,509 + 20,645]$) of speculative positions were long positions. The two situations are quite different. A higher probability exists that a top will occur when 94 percent of all speculative positions are long as opposed to 80 percent.

$$\%\,\text{Long} = \#\,\text{long contracts} \div (\#\,\text{long contracts} + \#\,\text{short contracts})$$

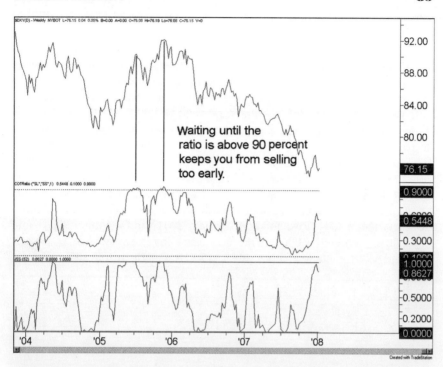

Waiting until the ratio is above 90 percent keeps you from selling too early.

FIGURE 5.12 Waiting until the ratio of speculative longs is also extreme (above 90 percent) can save you from acting on false signals provided by the COT Index
Source: Chart created on TradeStation®, the flagship product of TradeStation Technologies, Inc.

The chart in Figure 5.12 is the same as the chart in Figure 5.11, but with speculative longs expressed as a percentage of total speculative positions added to the bottom of the chart. Recall the example from May 2005. The COT Index reached 100 during the week that ended on May 20th and remained at 100 until the week that ended July 8th. Turning dollar bearish in May would have destroyed one's trading account. However, viewing the COT Index and the percent long ratio together more accurately reflects the psychological state of the market. When the COT Index first reaches 100, 81 percent of speculative contracts are long contracts. Long contracts expressed as a percentage of total contracts increases steadily until mid-July when the ratio reaches 92 percent.

Filtering the COT Index by looking at the percent long ratio results in a better understanding of where the market is in the never-ending oscillation of optimism and pessimism. I liken this to comparing the strength of two people who weigh different amounts. For example, a football offensive lineman who weighs 350 pounds is most likely stronger than a

200-pound swimmer in absolute terms. The lineman can bench-press 350 pounds whereas the swimmer can bench-press only 225 pounds. However, the swimmer is stronger relative to his weight since he can bench-press his own weight. I have a friend who weighs 190 pounds who can bench-press more than 400 pounds, so he would be considered stronger than the offensive lineman in both absolute and relative terms. Similarly, the most reliable turn signal occurs when positioning is extreme from both an absolute and relative perspective.

The ratio itself works especially well with the U.S. dollar. Plotted below the USD Index in Figure 5.13 is the percent long ratio since 1990. The dotted lines are at 80 and 20 percent. The ratio was below or very close to 20 percent twice in 1992 (lows made in January 1992 and September 1992), twice in 2004 (lows made in January 2004 and December 2004), and right now (September 2007). The ratio was above or very close to 80 percent in 1989 (top made in June 1989), 2001 (top made in July 2001), and for

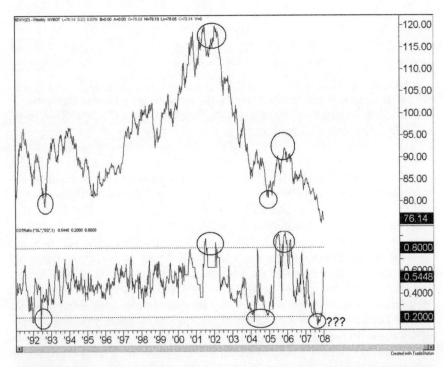

FIGURE 5.13 Looking only at the ratio of speculative longs to shorts for the DXY would have warned of very major turns
Source: Chart created on TradeStation®, the flagship product of TradeStation Technologies, Inc.

extended periods from May 2005 to March 2006 (a triple top of sorts was made during this time). The percent long ratio did not warn of every significant turn (*significant* in this sense would be at least multimonth), but it warned of very major turns.

Applying Percentiles to Ratios

Obviously, the goal is to have COT indicators that are not only timely but also reliable. Our arsenal includes the COT Index (which is calculated with the Composite COT) and the percent long ratio (speculative). I also look at the percent long ratio (commercial). Remember, there are three main characteristics of COT data that warn of a turn.

1. The difference between speculative and commercial positioning is large, usually the largest it has been in a certain period (13, 26, 52 weeks): COT Index at 0 or 100.
2. Speculative positioning is the most bullish at the top and most bearish at the bottom: Spec Ratio Index at 100 or 0.
3. Commercial positioning is the most bearish at the top and most bullish at the bottom: Comm Ratio Index at 0 or 100.

When these three things line up, the probability of a turn outweighs the risk that comes from giving back profits by staying in the trade. In this instance, it is wise to keep risk tight and/or examine the chart for a possible reversal trade. Figures 5.14 to 5.17 are charts of major currency pairs with the three COT indicators that I use: the COT Index, the Spec Ratio Index, and the Comm Ratio Index. Vertical lines indicate when the three indicators line up. In those instances, action is warranted.

OPEN INTEREST

I do not find much of an advantage to closely following open interest. That is not to say that open interest is useless; I simply do not believe any insight is gained that is not already gained by studying the commercial and speculative positioning. Open interest is a function of these two groups anyway. Also, there is no reason to junk up charts with indicators that are not needed. The traders that do follow open interest typically look for increasing open interest to gauge the strength of the trend. For example, increasing open interest and increasing price indicates a strong bull market. Similarly, increasing open interest and decreasing price indicates a strong

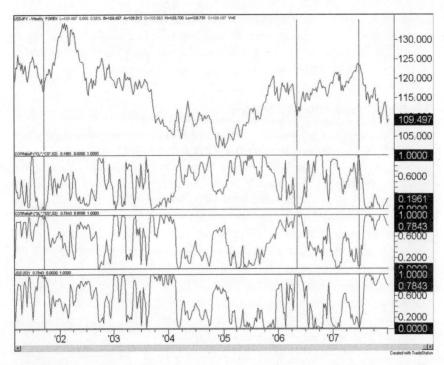

FIGURE 5.14 Some major turns in the USDJPY were signaled by the three COT indicators lining up at either 0 or 100
Source: Chart created on TradeStation®, the flagship product of TradeStation Technologies, Inc.

bear market. However, this analysis is backward looking in that it conveys to us what has happened, not what is likely to happen. In other words, just because open interest and price increased last week does not mean that the same will happen next week.

Also, notice in Figure 5.18 that open interest is extremely volatile in its fluctuations. In fact, tops in open interest occur on a three-month cycle. This is because the contract months for currency futures are March, June, September, and December. Trading for the specific contract month ends at 9:16 A.M. Central Time on the second business day immediately preceding the third Wednesday of the contract month (usually a Monday). The exception to this is the Canadian dollar, which stops trading at 9:16 A.M. Central Time on the business day immediately preceding the third Wednesday of the contract (usually a Tuesday). Futures traders must settle their contracts with either cash or by rolling over to the next contract month.

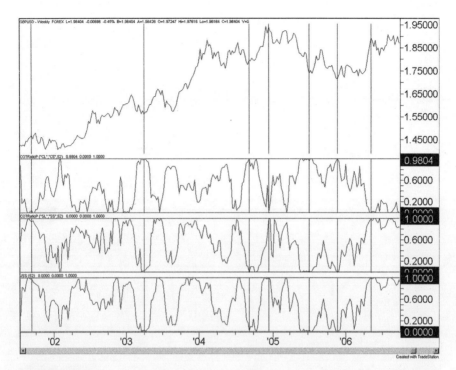

FIGURE 5.15 Some major turns in the GBPUSD were signaled by the three COT indicators lining up at either 0 or 100
Source: Chart created on TradeStation®, the flagship product of TradeStation Technologies, Inc.

The result is a short-term top in open interest every three months, usually during the second or third week of the contract month.

The tendency for open interest to run in three-month cycles makes it difficult to extract meaningful information, at least during the middle of the trend. However, major tops and bottoms do tend to occur when open interest is its highest within a specific period. In this sense, open interest is valuable at the same time as the Composite COT.

OTHER SENTIMENT INDICATORS

As mentioned previously, indicators derived from the COT data are the most useful in my opinion, but there are other options out there. This is a brief overview of the various sentiment and/or positioning indicators that I am aware of.

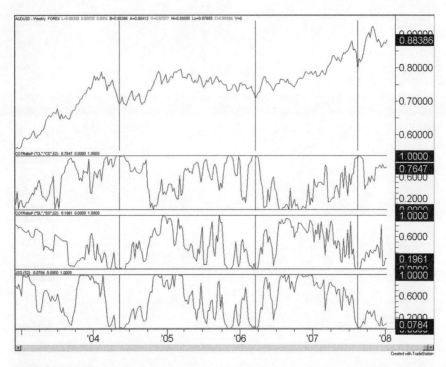

FIGURE 5.16 Some major turns in the AUDUSD were signaled by the three COT indicators lining up at either 0 or 100
Source: Chart created on TradeStation®, the flagship product of TradeStation Technologies, Inc.

FXCM Speculative Sentiment Index

The FXCM Speculative Sentiment Index (SSI) is based on proprietary customer flow information and is designed to recognize price trend breaks and reversals in the seven most popularly traded currency pairs. The SSI is a real-time snapshot of market sentiment measuring the open interest of small non-commercial forex market participants. The indicator is compiled using aggregate order flow information from FXCM's non-commercial clients. The size, breadth, and activity of the FXCM customer base provides a good representative sample of overall speculative behavior.

Every bank has this information but rarely discloses it due to its profitability in-house. FXCM remains neutral and does not trade against its clients; therefore, it is able to make this data publicly available. The absolute number of the ratio itself represents the amount by which long orders exceed short orders or vice versa. A negative number indicates that the majority of traders are net short while a positive number indicates that the

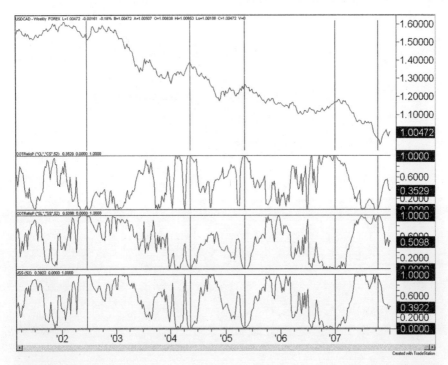

FIGURE 5.17 Some major turns in the USDCAD were signaled by the three COT indicators lining up at either 0 or 100
Source: Chart created on TradeStation®, the flagship product of TradeStation Technologies, Inc.

majority of traders are net long. For example, a EURUSD ratio of 2 means that long customer positions in the EURUSD exceed short positions by a ratio of 2 to 1. This list details how to interpret SSI. Figures 5.19 and 5.20 show daily charts accompanied by SSI.

- The SSI works as a contrarian indicator during trending markets.
- The flipping of the ratio is a more *accurate* signal of a turn in prices than extreme positioning.
- The SSI confirms the price action during range-bound markets.
- SSI moves *inversely* to price.
- Follow the slope of SSI; a change in slope indicates a change in trend.
- The other way of looking at speculative positioning is to view the percentage of open orders that are long.
- Net positioning = long orders + short orders.
- More than 50 percent long favors weakness.

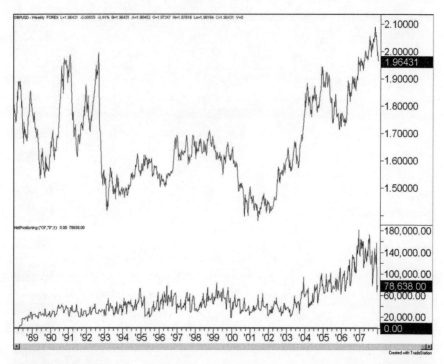

FIGURE 5.18 Open interest for the British pound is volatile, which makes discerning useful information difficult
Source: Chart created on TradeStation®, the flagship product of TradeStation Technologies, Inc.

- Less than 50 percent long favors strength.
- Higher net positioning means that more traders are entering the market.
- Higher net positioning suggests more confidence in the direction of the current trend.
- Many times a significant increase in net positioning precedes a bull market because many of the traders who entered the market are leaving their stop losses just above the current price action.
- Lower net positioning means that more discouraged traders are leaving the market.
- Rising prices with a big fall in net positioning is bearish because short covering is fueling the rising trend. When the short covering has ended, prices will likely decline.
- Lower net positioning suggests profit taking and therefore consolidation.
- Lower net positioning suggests higher risk aversion.

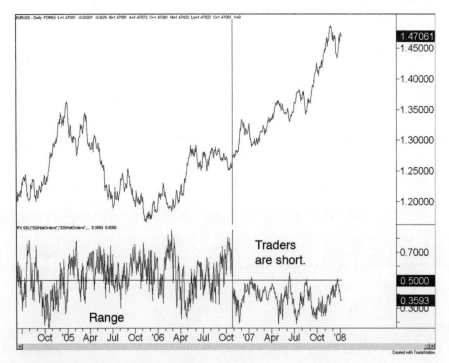

FIGURE 5.19 SSI on the EURUSD shows that as retail traders remain short, the pair continues to rally. The SSI is volatile during range periods
Source: Chart created on TradeStation®, the flagship product of TradeStation Technologies, Inc.

FXCM clients receive SSI readings twice a day, free of charge. The firm also offers a managed fund product based on SSI. For more information about the fund, see www.FXCMManagedFunds.com.

Daily Sentiment Index (from Jake Bernstein's trade-futures.com)

The Daily Sentiment Index (DSI) is a top-notch contrary opinion indicator. The DSI provides daily market sentiment readings on all active U.S. markets daily at 4:00 P.M Central Time. The DSI has become the standard in short-term market sentiment for futures traders. Currently in use by top banks, money managers, brokerage firms, professional traders, and speculators throughout the world, the DSI is used to spot and trade short-term market swings at extremes in small trader market sentiment. DSI is

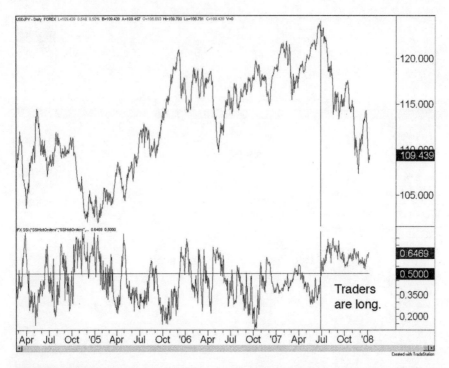

FIGURE 5.20 The same is true regardless of the pair traded. Retail traders flipped to a long position in July 2007, just when the USDJPY peaked at 124.13 and began a multimonth downtrend

Source: Chart created on TradeStation®, the flagship product of TradeStation Technologies, Inc.

supplied for a number of markets. See below for a brief introduction to the indicator and information on how to receive it.

- *How Supplied:* The DSI is available daily either in FAX form, daily voice recording, FTP, or Internet log-in to our web site.
- *Cost:* Call for pricing.
- *History:* Daily sentiment data history on 32 U.S. markets back to 1987 is provided at no additional charge to annual subscribers. Historical data cost is $99/year to nonsubscribers.
- *European Markets:* European DSI is available as well. Call for details.
- *Intra-day Sentiment:* This is available on selected U.S. markets. Call for details.
- *Meaning and Interpretation:* High percent bullish readings (i.e., 90 percent or higher) suggest that a short-term top is developing or has

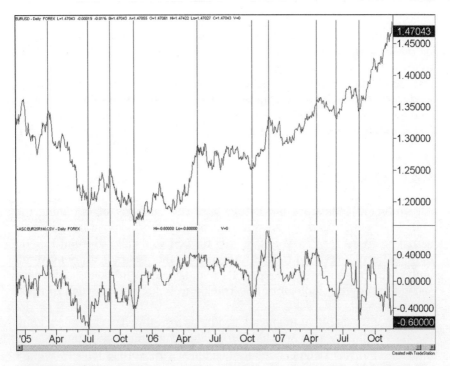

FIGURE 5.21 The risk reversal rate and the currency pair (the EURUSD, in this case) are positively correlated. Extremes in the risk reversal rate warn of short-term tops and bottoms in price
Source: Chart created on TradeStation®, the flagship product of TradeStation Technologies, Inc.

been made. Low percent bullish readings (i.e., 10 percent or lower) suggest that a short-term bottom is developing or has been made. Individual users have their own applications and interpretations. The service does not recommend trades, but provides the data which you may apply in your own trading program.

- *Subscriptions and Information:* Call 1-800-678-5253 or 847-446-0800 for subscriptions and additional information.

Risk Reversal Rates

Another useful tool that can be used to warn of extreme bullish or bearish psychology and therefore warn of market tops and bottoms is the risk reversal rate on currency options. The rate is updated as options prices update throughout the day, whereas the COT report is released once a week. The risk reversal rate calculates the difference between call option volatility and put option volatility on currency options. Call option volatility increases as options traders' bullishness increases and put option volatility increases as options traders' bearishness increases. Subtracting put volatility from call volatility produces the risk reversal rate. An extremely high rate, indicating extreme bullishness on the part of options traders, often leads to a top and reversal. Similarly, an extremely low rate, indicating extreme bearishness on the part of options traders, often leads to a bottom and reversal. The risk reversal rate for the EURUSD is shown in Figure 5.21.

CONCLUSION

All sentiment indicators move together. The methods of obtaining the bullish or bearish readings are different: actual reported positions for COT, actual positions for FXCM SSI, survey for DSI, and call rate—put rate on options for risk reversal rate. But the reason that the indicators move up and down is the same: psychology. Psychology moves markets, so it makes sense to study the indicators that track psychology if you wish to trade profitably.

Do not forget about the media headlines mentioned in Chapter 4. Look for the headlines with words like *surge* when the indicators in this chapter indicate a bullish extreme. Look for headlines with words such as *plummet* or *plunge*, when sentiment indicators indicate a bearish extreme. Headlines from daily publications with strong language indicate short-term sentiment extremes themselves. If these headlines appear when sentiment indicators also warn of sentiment extremes, then the signal is that much stronger.

CHAPTER 6

The Power of Technical Indicators

T he method that is referred to as *technical analysis* encompasses a wide array of techniques, including moving averages, oscillators, point and figure charting, candlesticks, time cycles, pivot points, trendlines, traditional chart patterns such as the head and shoulders, and tools derived from Fibonacci mathematics (which is the mathematical foundation for Elliott wave analysis). I will cover just a few of these indicators. There are so many indicators, and many new traders feel overwhelmed when it comes to deciding what technical tools to use for their trading. Technical analysis is only valuable if the person using it is disciplined. Once you develop a trading method robust enough that you feel comfortable risking real money, it is imperative to be consistent and stay with that strategy until further analysis suggests otherwise. Exploring and testing new methods is always important, but hastily changing your trading style because of a few bad trades destroys the advantage that technical analysis provides in the first place. That advantage is *objectivity*. The following hypothetical example sheds light on this matter.

A trader using a moving average to determine a directional bias might decide to take long trades if price is above the 21-day simple moving average and take short trades if price is below the 21-day simple moving average. There is nothing subjective about price being above or below the 21-day simple moving average. Price is either above or below the average: end of story. On the other hand, two traders could argue all day about the relationship between the Dow and the U.S. dollar. There is no consistent relationship, by the way; the Dow and the dollar sometimes advance together, decline together, and sometimes move in completely opposite

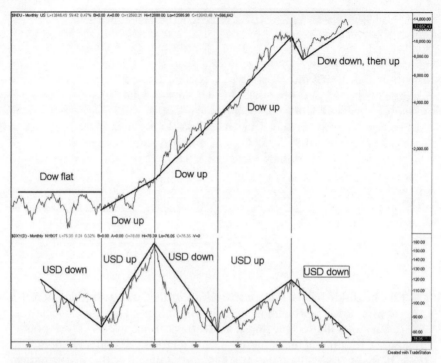

FIGURE 6.1 There is absolutely no consistent correlation between the Dow and the U.S. dollar
Source: Chart created on TradeStation®, the flagship product of TradeStation Technologies, Inc.

directions. See Figure 6.1. Both traders can sound convincing but at the end of the day, their opinion is just that. A moving average is objective, and the opinions of the traders arguing about the Dow and the U.S. dollar are subjective.

However, say that the moving average trader suffers a few bad trades in a ranging market. After all, a moving average is a trend-following indicator and moving average strategies get destroyed in range bound markets. The trader is discouraged and makes an emotion-based decision to switch methods. Remember, the decision to trade the moving average system was made rationally after testing was performed. The decision to change methods and try something else was made emotionally due to the pain of losing money. Of course, immediately after changing strategies, the market enters a trending period. The losses suffered would have been more than offset had the trader in this example had the discipline to stick with the moving average strategy.

Flip-flopping back and forth between technical methods is just as bad as trading based on backward looking fundamentals. Neither method leads to success. The biggest problem with both is lack of consistency and objectivity. I recently came across an article from Reuters titled "Stocks and dollar fall as economy, earnings sour." The first sentence of that article is "Stocks slipped and the dollar fell on Thursday after another batch of weak data suggested the economy faces further weakness." Three days earlier, a Thomson Financial article was titled "Dollar recovers against euro as investors turn to safe haven currencies." The first sentence of that article was "The dollar recovered firmly against the euro as falls in equity markets prompted investors to turn to safe-haven currencies." To summarize: On Monday, the dollar rallied and stocks fell because of a slowing economy. On Thursday, the dollar fell and stocks fell because of a slowing economy. There is nothing consistent or objective about that analysis nor is there anything consistent or objective about switching technical trading methods on a whim.

WHAT IS TECHNICAL ANALYSIS?

In trading, the trader is his own worst enemy. The emotional impulses from the limbic system win over the rationalization of the neocortex and the result, more often than not, is bad trading decisions (made emotionally, not rationally). Technical analysis helps us in that regard by providing objectivity. But what *is* technical analysis?

Technical analysis is the study of price action through pattern recognition and indicators in order to forecast future price action. Of course, there is no way to predict the next price move 100 percent of the time. Trading is a probability game and successful application of technical analysis alerts the trader to the highest probability move, whether that is up, down, or sideways. Collective psychology is the force behind every market move, and it is that psychology that shows up in a patterned way on the price chart (more on this in Chapter 7). This is where pattern recognition comes into play. Human history tends to repeat itself. Since markets are a manmade product, market action also repeats itself. The same patterns that showed up last year will show up next year, and the year after that, and . . . you get the idea. This remains the case as long as markets are a result of human interaction. Indicators include, among others, moving averages, pivot points, Bollinger bands, and oscillators. These indicators determine trend, gauge support and resistance, and warn if a market is too high or too low on a relative basis and might be ready to reverse course.

These indicators work because markets do trend and markets do reverse at optimistic and pessimistic extremes.

KEEP IT SIMPLE

One problem that traders, especially new traders, face is that there are so many indicators to use. Which ones should you use? Many free charting packages include at least a dozen or more indicators, and paid packages include many more. The charting package that I use provides hundreds of already programmed technical indicators. Traditionally, indicators are classified as either trending or range. Moving averages are often considered to work better in trending markets and oscillators such as RSI, and stochastics are considered to work better in range bound markets. Technical indicators are just a piece of the puzzle, along with sentiment indicators (see Chapter 5) and price patterns.

Using these tools together will improve your odds for success. Finally, there is no correct answer to the question, "What indicators should I use?" Trading is very personal, and you should use what you feel most comfortable with. I will show you how I use the indicators that I use, which hopefully will inspire your ideas.

WHAT TIME FRAMES TO USE?

A study of price data, technical analysis can be classified as a statistical study. Any statistician will tell you that the results become more reliable as more data is included in the study. In our case, the result is future price action (more specifically, a trading signal) and the data is past price action. An hourly chart will yield more reliable signals than a minute chart since the hourly chart includes much more data than a minute chart. Similarly, a daily chart will yield more reliable signals than an hourly chart, and a monthly chart will be more reliable than a daily, and so on. With this in mind, I find extremely short-term charts, which I consider anything under hourly bars, to be unfavorable.

Also, short-term trading increases the risk of making emotionally based decisions. For example, a swing trader risking 100 pips on a 1 lot trade is risking the same amount as a scalp trader risking 10 pips on 10 lots. Aside from the fact that the scalper's margin for error is far less, the scalper sees his P/L fluctuate in larger amounts. The opportunity to make or lose more in a shorter amount of time amplifies the greed and fear factor which in turn increases the likelihood of making a stupid trading decision.

Some traders thrive in such an environment, but most do not. I know that my personality is too impulsive to scalp successfully, which is why I refrain from making trading decisions based on charts shorter than hourly bars.

SUPPORT AND RESISTANCE

Before we go any further, it is vital to present the foundation for all of technical analysis: support and resistance. *Support* is an area below the market price where buying overcomes selling (Figure 6.2). *Resistance* is an area above the market price where selling overcomes buying (Figure 6.3). Support and resistance are estimated in different ways, including previous highs and lows, Fibonacci retracements and extensions, pivot points,

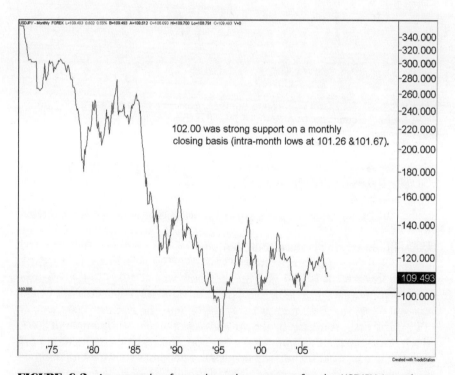

FIGURE 6.2 An example of round number support for the USDJPY just above 100.00
Source: Chart created on TradeStation®, the flagship product of TradeStation Technologies, Inc.

FIGURE 6.3   An example of round number resistance for the GBPUSD at 2.0000
Source: Chart created on TradeStation®, the flagship product of TradeStation Technologies, Inc.

moving averages, and sometimes round psychological levels such as USDJPY 100.00 or GBPUSD 2.0000.

Properly identifying support and resistance is critical to becoming a successful trader because a big part of market timing depends on buying close to support and selling close to resistance. Also, support and resistance should be viewed as a zone, not a point. For example, 101.00/102.00 was a long-term support zone for the USDJPY. The 1993 low was at 101.10, the 1999 low was at 101.26, and the 2005 low was at 101.67. Similarly, the zone surrounding 2.0000 was resistance for the GBPUSD as the 1991 high was at 1.9990, the 1992 high was at 2.0035, and the January 2007 was at 1.9914. The pair eventually broke through resistance in the summer of 2007, which brings up another point about support and resistance. Once support or resistance is broken, the level in question becomes its opposite. In other words, former support becomes resistance and former resistance becomes support. See Figures 6.4 and 6.5 for examples of this.

Understanding not just where but also why specific price levels act as support or resistance breeds the confidence required to trade

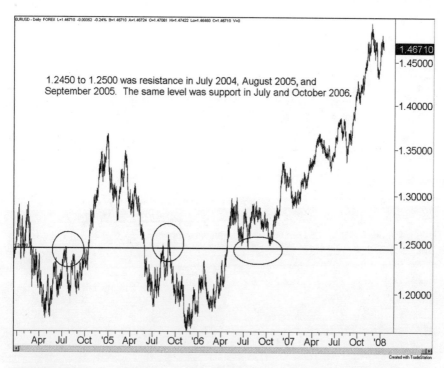

1.2450 to 1.2500 was resistance in July 2004, August 2005, and September 2005. The same level was support in July and October 2006.

FIGURE 6.4 The 1.2500 level was resistance in July 2004, August 2005, and September 2005. That same level became support in July and October 2006
Source: Chart created on TradeStation®, the flagship product of TradeStation Technologies, Inc.

successfully. Successful traders are confident in their approach because they understand it.

Support and resistance are so for a reason. These are not just arbitrary points on a chart. There is a psychology behind why support and resistance are where they are. Consider the USDCAD chart in Figure 6.5. In November 2004, many traders bought and sold near 1.1700. Those who bought were delighted with themselves as the USDCAD traded higher over the next several months. Those who sold were feeling pain as their losses mounted. When the price came back to the 1.1700 level in October 2005, the traders who were long protected their positions by buying more, and the traders who were short were ecstatic to get out of the trade at breakeven by covering their shorts. Both groups bought in this instance, and 1.1700 was support again. However, bearish sentiment ensured that the buying was not sufficient enough to hold 1.1700. As price, now below 1.1700, trades back to 1.1700, those long now decide to get out at breakeven and bears returned

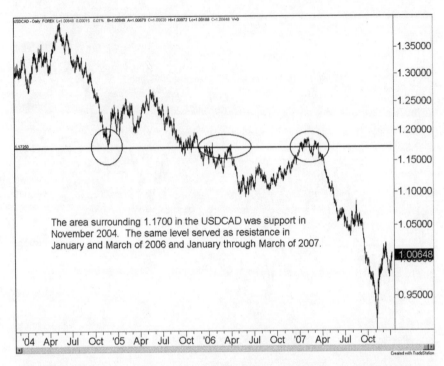

The area surrounding 1.1700 in the USDCAD was support in November 2004. The same level served as resistance in January and March of 2006 and January through March of 2007.

FIGURE 6.5 The 1.1700 level in the USDCAD was support in November 2004 and served as resistance in January and March of 2006 as well as January and March of 2007
Source: Chart created on TradeStation®, the flagship product of TradeStation Technologies, Inc.

to sell at the same level that they themselves had sold at before. Now, both groups are sellers and the price plummets.

DETERMINING A BIAS

Patterns and market form are covered in Chapter 7. At this time, we'll move to technical indicators. The most important function that technical indicators serve is presenting a point of reference from which to trade against. Whether a moving average or a pivot point, both tools make a division between bullish and bearish. Even oscillators such as RSI provide a reference point from which to trade against. Oscillators are different because they do not provide actual price points, but they do describe the current market condition. Does the indicator support a bullish or bearish bias? Are conditions overbought or oversold? These are the questions that indicators help answer.

Moving Averages

Moving averages are the most widely used technical indicators and probably the simplest to understand. There are different kinds of moving averages but the most common are the simple moving average (SMA) and the exponential moving average (EMA). An SMA is just the average of a specified body of data. For example, a 10-period SMA is the sum of the last 10 prices (usually closing prices) divided by 10.

The calculation for an EMA is much more complicated. Some technicians prefer the EMA to the SMA, arguing that it decreases lag time because it assigns more weight to the most recent price. Although the SMA uses just the number of periods specified in its calculation, the EMA uses all of the data on the chart (if you are using a 10-day EMA and looking at a three-year chart, all three years of data will be in that EMA). How does this work? As mentioned, the EMA calculation is more complicated than that of the SMA.

$$\text{EMA(current)} = \text{EMA(previous)} + \text{SmoothingFactor}$$
$$\times \text{(Price} - \text{EMA[previous])}$$
$$\text{SmoothingFactor} = 2 \div (1 + n)$$
$$n = \text{periods}$$
$$\text{If } n = 10, \text{ then the multiplier} = 2 \div 11 = .181818.$$

Since the current EMA is calculated from the previous EMA, which is calculated from the previous EMA, which is calculated from the previous EMA, and so on, every price on the chart is included in the current EMA. Older prices have less of an effect on the current EMA than newer prices do, but they do have an effect, nonetheless. The calculation is similar to the passing down of genes in a family. My genes are very similar to my parents, less similar to my grandparents, and even less similar to my great grandparents (but there is a similarity nonetheless), and so on.

Is an EMA really better than an SMA? The calculation is more complicated, but that doesn't mean anything. In fact, simplicity is often rewarded in trading. A 13-day SMA and 13-day EMA are plotted on the EURUSD chart in Figure 6.6. The EMA is usually closer to price than the SMA since more weight is given to the most recent prices. As a result, the EMA provides quicker signals, but this can also lead to more false signals. Is the payoff worth it? Let's find out by running some basic optimization tests.

The tests are of single moving average crossovers using EURUSD data from January 1998 until October 2007. Figure 6.6 shows the chart with

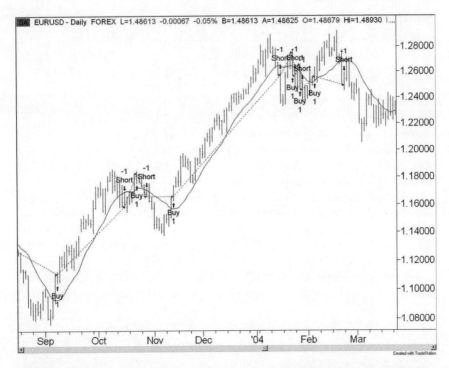

FIGURE 6.6 Buy when price crosses above the moving average and sell when price crosses below the moving average. There is no simpler trending strategy and it works well
Source: Chart created on TradeStation®, the flagship product of TradeStation Technologies, Inc.

examples of actual buy and sell signals, and Table 6.1 details the test results. The rules are as follows:

1. If the close is greater than the MA, then buy at 1 pip above the high.
2. If the close is less than the MA, then sell at 1 pip below the low. (Buying 1 pip above the high and selling 1 pip below the low acts as a filter for false signals.)

For the daily tests, I ran crossovers for periods 10 to 21 (2 weeks to about a month). See Table 6.1.

Interestingly, the SMA results are better than the EMA results. The SMA is better when considering percent profitable and net profit. Win/loss ratio and max drawdown are about the same. For both types of moving average, 13 days was the best input when only considering profit.

TABLE 6.1 The best parameter for both the SMA and EMA daily tests is 13. Overall, the SMA results are better

SMA	Total Trades	Percent Profitable	Win/Loss Ratio	Net Profit	Max Intraday Drawdown
13	250	33.20	2.39	$ 32,305.50	$ (20,970.00)
14	242	31.40	2.57	$ 29,858.50	$ (17,447.50)
11	274	34.31	2.17	$ 26,292.50	$ (23,433.50)
12	264	33.71	2.20	$ 22,467.50	$ (23,913.50)
17	230	26.52	3.03	$ 15,532.50	$ (16,310.00)
16	236	26.69	2.94	$ 12,576.50	$ (16,783.50)
15	240	29.17	2.59	$ 11,954.50	$ (17,770.00)
18	226	26.11	2.96	$ 8,168.50	$ (21,930.00)
19	226	26.55	2.82	$ 3,810.50	$ (22,370.00)
10	300	33.33	1.99	$ 1,352.50	$ (25,393.50)
21	214	25.70	2.88	$ 337.50	$ (25,810.00)
20	226	24.78	2.82	$ (10,974.50)	$ (25,810.00)

EMA	Total Trades	Percent Profitable	Win/Loss Ratio	Net Profit	Max Intraday Drawdown
13	259	28.19	2.77	$ 16,620.50	$ (17,650.00)
11	289	30.10	2.40	$ 8,245.50	$ (20,750.00)
14	255	27.06	2.75	$ 4,577.50	$ (19,150.00)
21	217	26.73	2.82	$ 4,488.50	$ (23,330.00)
20	227	26.43	2.82	$ 2,141.50	$ (23,330.00)
12	281	28.47	2.51	$ 1,707.50	$ (21,340.00)
15	255	27.06	2.67	$ (546.50)	$ (19,150.00)
18	245	25.71	2.78	$ (6,350.50)	$ (21,570.00)
10	311	30.23	2.21	$ (7,056.50)	$ (22,540.00)
19	239	25.52	2.79	$ (7,552.50)	$ (23,330.00)
16	255	25.88	2.71	$ (8,510.50)	$ (20,550.00)
17	249	25.70	2.70	$ (11,470.50)	$ (23,290.00)

For the weekly tests, I ran crossovers for periods 4 to 12 (roughly 1 to 3 months). See Table 6.2.

The weekly results are very close. The SMA results are more consistent as the difference in performance for the EMA tests varies.

Much more thorough testing would be required in order to confidently conclude whether one type of moving average is better than the other. Still, these basic tests suggest one possible conclusion: There is no better moving average. One might work better in some situations than the other and vice versa. That is the nature of markets; no one single indicator is going to offer the holy grail all the time.

TABLE 6.2	The best parameter for the SMA and EMA weekly tests is probably 4. There is not much of a difference between the EMA and SMA weekly tests, although the SMA tests are more consistent

SMA	All: Total Trades	All: Percent Profitable	All: Win/Loss Ratio	All: Net Profit	All: Max Intraday Drawdown
4	83	36.14	2.62	$ 41,350.00	$ (17,470.00)
5	79	39.24	2.27	$ 38,695.50	$ (14,270.00)
10	51	41.18	2.26	$ 36,741.00	$ (16,050.00)
7	69	42.03	1.98	$ 32,596.50	$ (15,590.00)
11	51	41.18	2.12	$ 31,054.00	$ (16,050.00)
12	47	40.43	2.19	$ 30,324.50	$ (20,082.50)
9	59	40.68	2.03	$ 27,747.50	$ (14,730.00)
8	65	40.00	2.02	$ 27,352.50	$ (15,590.00)
6	75	40.00	1.90	$ 23,042.50	$ (15,590.00)

EMA	All: Total Trades	All: Percent Profitable	All: Win/Loss Ratio	All: Net Profit	All: Max Intraday Drawdown
9	52	44.23	2.18	$ 41,114.00	$ (16,050.00)
4	82	36.59	2.58	$ 40,722.50	$ (14,270.00)
10	46	36.96	2.95	$ 39,636.00	$ (17,250.00)
11	44	38.64	2.74	$ 39,243.00	$ (17,250.00)
12	46	36.96	2.80	$ 36,763.00	$ (17,250.00)
8	60	41.67	1.99	$ 28,697.00	$ (16,050.00)
6	70	41.43	1.85	$ 24,389.50	$ (14,270.00)
5	78	37.18	2.10	$ 21,892.50	$ (14,270.00)
7	70	38.57	1.84	$ 12,875.50	$ (18,850.00)

Pivot Points

As previously mentioned in this chapter, trading requires reference points (support and resistance) from which to enter the market, place stops, and take profits. One tool that actually provides potential support and resistance and therefore helps minimize risk is the pivot point and its derivatives. Originally employed by floor traders on equity and futures exchanges, pivot points have proved exceptionally useful in the FX market. Pivot points can be calculated for any time frame. The previous period's prices are used to calculate the pivot point for the next period, as follows:

$$\text{Pivot point for current} = \text{high(previous)} + \text{low(previous)}$$
$$+ \text{close(previous)} \div 3$$

The pivot point is then used to calculate estimated support and resistance for the current trading period, as shown here:

Resistance $1 = (2 \times$ pivot point$) -$ low(previous period)

Support $1 = (2 \times$ pivot point$) -$ high(previous period)

Resistance $2 = ($pivot point $-$ support $1) +$ resistance 1

Support $2 =$ pivot point $- ($resistance $1 -$ support $1)$

Resistance $3 = ($pivot point $-$ support $2) +$ resistance 2

Support $3 =$ pivot point $- ($resistance $2 -$ support $2)$

In order to fully understand how well pivot points can work, I compiled statistics for the EUR/USD on how distant each high and low has been from each calculated resistance (R1, R2, R3) and support level (S1, S2, S3). To do the calculations yourself,

1. Calculate the pivot points, support levels, and resistance levels for x number of days.
2. Subtract the support pivot points from the actual low of the day (low – S1, low – S2, low – S3).
3. Subtract the resistance pivot points from the actual high of the day (high – R1, high – R2, high – R3).
4. Calculate the average for each difference.

I conducted this study in October 2006; data used in the study is EURUSD daily high, low, and close from January 1999 until October 2006.

- The actual low is, on average, 1 pip below Support 1.
- The actual high is, on average, 1 pip below Resistance 1.
- The actual low is, on average, 53 pips above Support 2.
- The actual high is, on average, 53 pips below Resistance 2.
- The actual low is, on average, 158 pips above Support 3.
- The actual high is, on average, 159 pips below Resistance 3.

The statistics indicate that the calculated pivot points of S1 and R1 are a decent gauge for the actual high and low of the trading day. Going a step further, I calculated the number of days that the low was lower than each S1, S2, and S3 and the number of days that the high was higher than each R1, R2, and R3.

- The actual low has been lower than S1 892 times, or 44 percent of the time.

- The actual high has been higher than R1 853 times, or 42 percent of the time.
- The actual low has been lower than S2 342 times, or 17 percent of the time.
- The actual high has been higher than R2 354 times, or 17 percent of the time.
- The actual low has been lower than S3 63 times, or 3 percent of the time.
- The actual high has been higher than R3 52 times, or 3 percent of the time.

This information is obviously useful to any trader. If you know that the pair slips below S1 44 percent of the time, then you can place a stop below S1 with confidence, knowing that probability is on your side. In addition, you may want to take profits just below R1 because you know that the high for the day exceeds R1 only 42 percent of the time. Again the probabilities are with you. It is important to understand that these are probabilities and not certainties. On average, the high is 1 pip below R1 and exceeds R1 42 percent of the time. This does not mean that the high will exceed R1 4 days out of the next 10 nor does it mean that the high is always going to be 1 pip below R1. The power in this information lies in the fact that you can confidently gauge potential support and resistance ahead of time, have reference points to place stops and limits, and, most importantly, limit risk while putting yourself in a position to profit.

Remember, the pivot point concept can be applied to any period. A day trader can use daily data to calculate the pivot points each day, a swing trader can use weekly data to calculate the pivot points for each week (Figure 6.7), and a position trader can use monthly data to calculate the pivot points at the beginning of each month (Figure 6.8). Even an investor can use yearly data to approximate significant levels for the coming year. The trading philosophy remains the same regardless of the time frame. That is, the calculated pivot points give the trader an idea of where support and resistance are for the coming period.

Pivot Zones

In *The Logical Trader*, Mark Fisher introduces the pivot zone. Rather than using just one point (high + low + close) ÷ 3 to determine a period's pivot, Fisher calculates two points.

1. Calculate the regular pivot (high + low + close) ÷ 3.
2. Calculate a second number (high + low) ÷ 2.

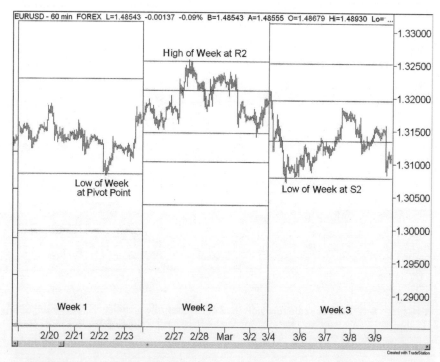

FIGURE 6.7 The pivot point, R2, and S2 pinpoint turns in the EURUSD quite often, as the example in this chart illustrates

Source: Chart created on TradeStation®, the flagship product of TradeStation Technologies, Inc.

3. Find the difference between the two numbers.

4. Add the absolute value of the difference in order to find the PivotHigh (PH).

5. Add the absolute value of the difference in order to find the PivotLow (PL).

The result is a rolling pivot zone rather than just a pivot point. See Figure 6.9 for an illustration of weekly pivot zones.

The pivot zone provides an area of reference from which to be bullish or bearish. If price is above the pivot zone, then a bullish bias is warranted with a stop below the pivot zone. If price is below the pivot zone, then a bearish bias is warranted with a stop above the pivot zone. Price often ranges within the pivot zone. By only playing breakouts from the pivot zone, buying above PH and selling below PL, you have a method to avoid frustrating whipsaw market action.

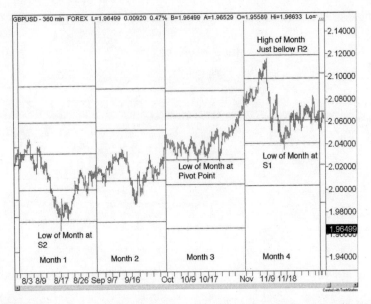

FIGURE 6.8 Larger scale turns often occur at monthly pivot levels for the GBPUSD
Source: Chart created on TradeStation®, the flagship product of TradeStation Technologies, Inc.

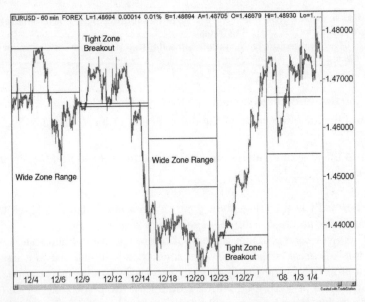

FIGURE 6.9 Not just where the pivot zone is, but also how wide the zone is, can aid in your trading
Source: Chart created on TradeStation®, the flagship product of TradeStation Technologies, Inc.

The width of the pivot zone offers clues as to what type of market to expect. A tight pivot zone warns of a breakout period and a wide pivot zone indicates a higher probability of a range bound period. If you think about the calculation of the pivot zone, it makes sense that tight and wide zones warn of breakouts or ranges. The width of the zone depends on where the close of the previous period is in relationship to that period's high and low. If the close is exactly equidistant to the high and the low, then the PH and the PL will be equal and the pivot zone will be just 1 pip. The nearer that the close is to the high or the low, the wider the zone will be. For example, a strong bull move results in a closing price near the high of the period. The pivot zone for the next period will be wide, indicating increased potential for a range bound market that period. In markets, periods of trend are followed by periods of consolidation and the width of the pivot zone reflects that.

Rolling Pivot Zone

Another one of Fisher's trading tools is the rolling pivot zone. In a way, it is a combination of a moving average and a pivot zone. The only difference between a regular pivot zone and a rolling pivot zone is that the rolling pivot zone uses more than one period's data in its calculation. Instead of using the high, low, and close from the previous period, the rolling pivot zone uses the highest high of the last x number of periods, the lowest low of the last x number of periods, and the close (same as the regular pivot zone). Fisher mentions that he will use a three-day rolling pivot zone. For a three-day rolling pivot zone, use the highest high of the last three days, the lowest low of the last three days, and the close from the last day. The rolling pivot zone is great for trailing stops, as Figure 6.10 illustrates. If you choose to use a rolling pivot, then experiment with different parameters, such as a three-, four-, or five-day rolling pivot. Similar to a moving average, a longer lookback period is less timely but more reliable. If you are a scalper, then experiment with 12- or 24-hour rolling pivots.

Oscillators

Whereas moving averages and pivot points (including rolling pivots) are plotted with price, oscillators are plotted below (or above) price. There are two types of oscillators: those with limits that indicate whether price is overbought or oversold and those without limits. Those with limits are referred to as *banded* because of the bands that denote overbought and oversold. Those without limits are referred to as *centered* because the oscillator fluctuates above and below a center line. However, banded oscillators also fluctuate around a center line so differentiating between the two types of oscillators with these names is misleading. As such, we'll refer to the two types as *limit* and *no-limit*.

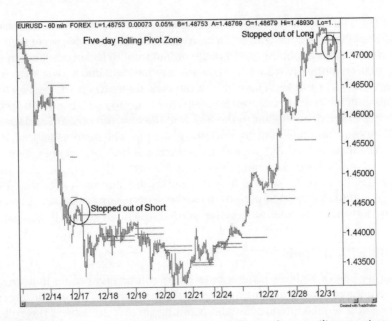

FIGURE 6.10   A five-day rolling pivot zone can be used as a trailing stop in order to lock in profits
Source: Chart created on TradeStation®, the flagship product of TradeStation Technologies, Inc.

There is very little difference visually between price oscillators. All move up at the same time and all move down at the same time. All price oscillators are calculated from the same thing: price. This sounds painfully obvious. However, many new traders feel the need to use a multitude of oscillators. The result is dedicating too much attention to the indicators and not enough to price action itself. Still, oscillators are valuable tools and should be implemented as part of a successful trading strategy.

Momentum and Rate of Change   Momentum, the most basic oscillator, is the arithmetic change in price over a specified period of time. If you were calculating a 13-day momentum, then just subtract the closing price of 13 days ago from today's closing price.

$$\text{Momentum} = \text{price(current)} - \text{price}(x \text{ periods ago})$$

The most important feature of momentum is the relation of the indicator to the zero line. A reading above 0 indicates positive price change, and a reading below 0 indicates negative price change. For example, 13 period momentum crossing above the 0 line indicates that the closing price of the current period is now greater than the closing price 13 days ago. This represents a shift in power: Bulls are in control. The trend strengthens and the momentum line strays further from the zero line until the trend reaches a point of exhaustion. At this point, a momentum extreme is registered as the indicator has reached a peak (or trough) and turns down (or up). Once again, the model of optimism and pessimism oscillating back and forth is exhibited.

Momentum is often used interchangeably with rate of change. On intraday charts, there is no difference visually between the two, but there is an important difference on long-term charts. Rate of change is the geometric change in price over a specified period of time.

$$\text{Rate of change} = \text{price(current)} \div \text{price}(x \text{ periods ago})$$

Longer-term charts should always be looked at on a logarithmic scale. On a log scale, price change is plotted as a percentage rather than an absolute number. On an arithmetic scale, a movement of 1 to 2 is the same as a movement of 10 to 11. Going from 1 to 2 is a 100 percent change, or doubling in price. Going from 10 to 11 is just a 10 percent change. On a logarithmic scale, a movement of 10 to 11 would be displayed as 1/10th the change of a movement of 1 to 2. This makes sense. Figures 6.11 and 6.12

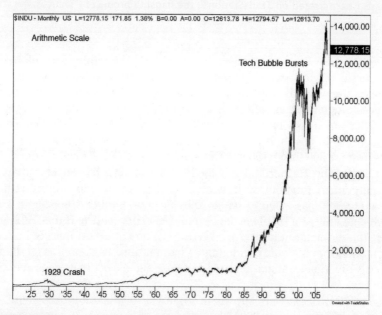

FIGURE 6.11 On the arithmetic scale, the 1929 crash looks inconsequential but the burst of the tech bubble looks catastrophic
Source: Chart created on TradeStation®, the flagship product of TradeStation Technologies, Inc.

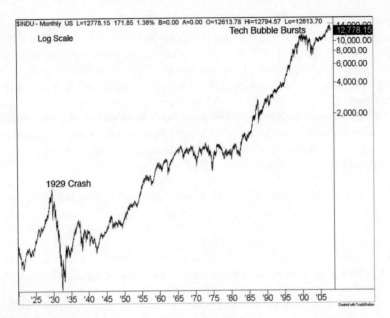

FIGURE 6.12 The log scale puts things in perspective
Source: Chart created on TradeStation®, the flagship product of TradeStation Technologies, Inc.

are of the Dow Jones Industrial Average (DJIA) monthly chart plotted on arithmetic and log scales. On the arithmetic scale, a move from 100 to 200 appears the same as a move from 10,000 to 10,100. Obviously, the former move is much more significant and the logarithmic scale captures that.

What does this have to do with an indicator? If you are measuring momentum in absolute terms, then you would conclude that a EURUSD rally from 1.0000 to 1.1000 is the same as a EURUSD rally from 1.3000 to 1.4000. The former move was 10 percent and the latter move was 7.7 percent. A momentum indicator displays these two moves as being equal (1,000 pips) when in reality they are not. On the other hand, a rate of change indicator displays the two moves in percentage terms. At market tops, the momentum indicator overstates momentum. At market bottoms, the momentum indicator understates momentum. The result is a failure to identify divergence at market tops and false signals of divergence at market bottoms.

The EURUSD chart shown in Figure 6.13 illustrates this point perfectly. At the December 2004 high, the rate of change indicator accurately identifies bearish divergence but the momentum indicator does not. If you were following the momentum indicator (arithmetic) rather than the rate

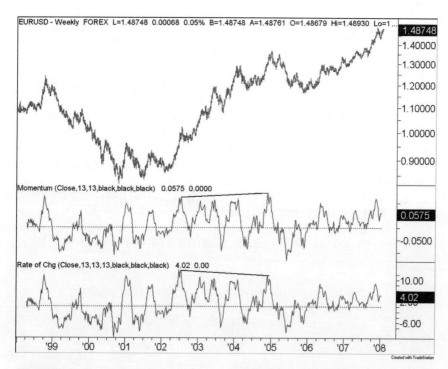

FIGURE 6.13 Momentum (arithmetic) fails to identify divergence at the December 2004 top, but rate of change (log or geometric) does identify the divergence
Source: Chart created on TradeStation®, the flagship product of TradeStation Technologies, Inc.

of change indicator (geometric), you would have missed this important signal. As mentioned, you will not be able to tell a difference between the momentum and rate of change indicators on short time frames because the absolute change and percentage change in price are roughly the same when viewing, for example, 15-minute or hourly price changes. The difference is magnified as you begin to look at longer time intervals. For this reason, I make a habit of always using the rate of change indicator rather than the momentum indicator. In this book, from now on, I will use momentum in a general sense although the indicator on the chart will always be rate of change.

Divergence

As tempting as it is to fade a momentum extreme, the outcome is usually costly. Price extremes rarely coincide with momentum extremes. Price can and often does continue in the direction of the underlying trend, although at a slower rate of change. In other words, momentum slows but direction does not. In an uptrend, the result is a series of higher highs in price but lower highs in momentum. In a downtrend, the result is a series of lower lows in price but higher lows in momentum. What I have just described is *divergence* (price and indicator diverge). Bearish divergence occurs at market tops, and bullish divergence occurs at market bottoms. Divergence is present at every turn, but divergence does not always lead to a turn. Think about that for a moment. Divergence warns that the trend is reaching a point of exhaustion and that probability of a market turn has increased.

In Figure 6.14, a 13-week rate of change is plotted below the EURUSD weekly chart. A momentum extreme is reached in July 2002 when the EURUSD traded to 1.0206. As it turned out, the momentum extreme was reached in the middle of a trend that saw the EURUSD rally from .8227 to

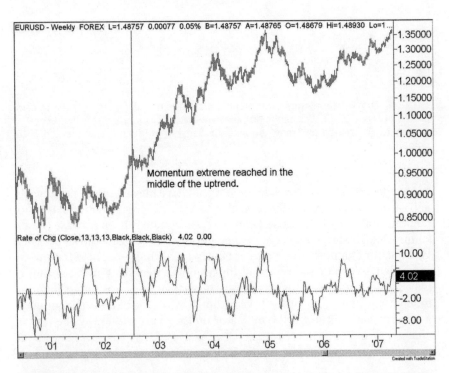

FIGURE 6.14 A momentum extreme announces that a bull trend is at its beginning or middle, not its end

Source: Chart created on TradeStation®, the flagship product of TradeStation Technologies, Inc.

1.3666 in four years and two months. There were numerous pauses and corrections along the way, all of which were preceded by bearish divergence. However, a top of significant proportion was not reached until December 2004. This is a perfect example of how divergence is present at every turn, but divergence does not always lead to a turn.

Divergence warns of trend reversal but does not always result in trend reversal. Understanding why divergence occurs is key to understanding market behavior in general. The strongest momentum reading usually occurs either at the beginning or the middle of the trend, not the end. The DJIA monthly chart with 12-month rate of change in Figure 6.15 best exemplifies this dynamic. The greatest rate of change (12 months) occurred during the 12 months that followed the July 1932 bottom. From July 1932 to June 1933, the Dow gained 129 percent. No 12-month period since has seen a gain of that magnitude (in percentage terms). Selling at the momentum extreme in June 1933 would not have been a very good idea. The next decent selling opportunity for the Dow would have been March 1937. Bearish divergence warned of this turn (see Figure 6.15).

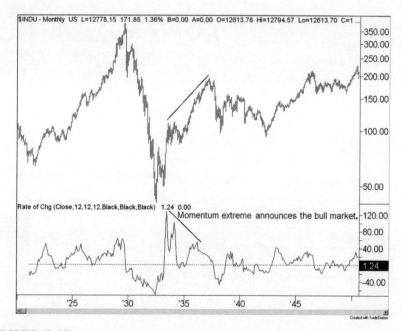

FIGURE 6.15 The momentum extreme in the Dow that was registered in the mid-1930s gave way to the biggest equity bull market of all time
Source: Chart created on TradeStation®, the flagship product of TradeStation Technologies, Inc.

Using Momentum Extremes to Trade a Reversal

Let's expand on how to use momentum extremes in trading. Again, momentum extremes almost always occur at the beginning or middle of a move. If this is the case, then the correct decision is to trade in the direction of the momentum extreme. Most retail traders fade these extremes and lose money in the process. Figure 6.16 is of the EURUSD daily chart with 13-day rate of change plotted below. Following the December 2004 top at 1.3666, the pair plummeted and by January 18, 2005, the 13-day rate of change was at –4.50, the lowest reading since August 2002. The EURUSD closed at 1.3020 on January 18th. Many traders probably tried to fade this momentum extreme and by February 7th the pair had slid to 1.2730. A corrective rally followed and ended at 1.3480 on March 11th. With the understanding that the momentum extreme in January was bearish for EURUSD, a savvy trader was looking for opportunities to sell rallies such as the one into the March high. The rest of 2005 saw the pair fall nearly 2,000 pips.

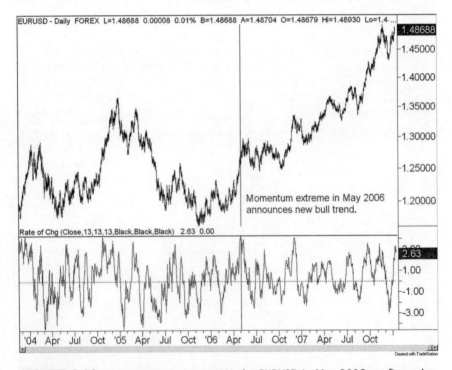

FIGURE 6.16 A momentum extreme in the EURUSD in May 2006 confirms that the decline from the 2004 high is complete
Source: Chart created on TradeStation®, the flagship product of TradeStation Technologies, Inc.

The next example (see Figure 6.16 again) is also of the EURUSD but from the bullish side. The decline that began at 1.3666 ended at 1.1640 in November 2005. On May 3, 2006, the 13-day EURUSD rate of change stood at 4.30. This was the highest reading since December 2003. The May 3rd closing price was 1.2630. Much like the previous example, many traders probably tried to fade the momentum extreme only to see the rally extend to 1.2970 by May 15th. As it turned out, the momentum extreme in May 2006 was the kickoff for the EURUSD rally that would eventually challenge 1.5000.

I have used the term *momentum extreme* a lot, so a definition is in order. A momentum extreme occurs when rate of change is greatest (plus or minus) over a specified amount of time. The amount of time specified and the power of the signal are directly correlated. In other words, a three-year momentum extreme is more powerful than a one-year momentum extreme. Of course, this technique can be applied to any time frame. For example, a 120-hour rate of change covers five days. In this instance, you are looking for a five-day momentum extreme in order to determine a bias. If using momentum to trade reversals, then the momentum extreme must be made in the direction opposite the preceding trend. For example, Figure 6.17 is of the USDCAD daily chart with 13-day rate of change. The pair had clearly been in a downtrend for some time, but a momentum extreme was made on November 6, 2007. This is not a signal to get bearish USDCAD, because the USDCAD had been declining for some time. However, notice that a bullish momentum extreme was made on November 23rd. This is a valid reversal signal since the extreme occurs in the direction opposite the previous trend.

FANCY MOMENTUM INDICATORS AND OVERBOUGHT/OVERSOLD

Simpler indicators such as moving averages or rate of change are very useful, but most traders feel the need to use fancier indicators such as RSI and/or stochastics. These indicators have the ability to label a market overbought or oversold. I urge caution in using these indicators.

Relative Strength Index

J. Welles Wilder, Jr., developed the Relative Strength Index (RSI) and introduced the indicator to the trading community in *New Concepts in Technical Trading Systems* in 1978. RSI is probably the most popular oscillator among traders, and for good reason in my opinion. RSI is basically an

FIGURE 6.17 The USDCAD trend had been down for some time so the bearish momentum extreme indicates a bottom, not the middle of the trend. On the contrary, the bullish momentum extreme that occurred in November 2007 is a valid reversal signal
Source: Chart created on TradeStation®, the flagship product of TradeStation Technologies, Inc.

improved version of momentum (see Figure 6.18 for a comparison of the two indicators). There are two obvious benefits to using RSI rather than or in addition to rate of change. An RSI line is less erratic than a simple rate of change (momentum) line, and an RSI line provides limits of 0 and 100 so that the trader can gauge overbought and oversold levels.

Wilder expanded on the simple momentum calculation in formulating RSI. Details of the calculation are below.

$$\text{RSI} = 100 - (100 \div [1 + \text{RS}])$$
$$\text{Initial RS} = \text{average gain} \div \text{average loss}$$
$$\text{Subsequent RS} = ([\text{previous average gain} \times (n - 1)]$$
$$+ \text{current gain}) \div n/([\text{previous average loss}$$
$$\times (n - 1)] + \text{current loss}) \div n$$
$$\text{Average gain} = \text{total gains} \div n$$
$$\text{Average loss} = \text{total losses} \div n$$
$$n = \text{number of periods}$$

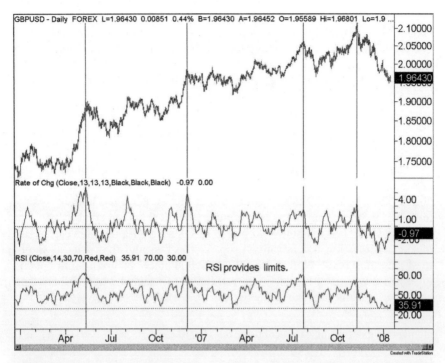

FIGURE 6.18 More or less the same indicator, RSI provides limits that label a market overbought or oversold
Source: Chart created on TradeStation®, the flagship product of TradeStation Technologies, Inc.

As you can see, the calculation is far more complex than simply rate of change or momentum. Instead of simply dropping the last data point $(n + 1)$ in the calculation, Wilder developed RS (relative strength). Think back to the exponential moving average equation and the family analogy. The current RS uses the previous average gain and average loss in its calculation. Each previous RS uses the average gain and average loss previous to it. You get the picture. RS is a rolling, continuous calculation. In theory, all of the data in the history of the instrument has an effect on the current RS reading. In reality, the effect of price changes from far back diminishes as time progresses to the point that the price changes are not noticeable. In any case, the result is a smoother line than if the calculation simply dropped off the last data point $(n + 1)$.

The other significant improvement is the presence of limits: 0 and 100. If the average gain is 0, then RSI would be 0. If the average loss is 0, then RSI would be 100. This does not happen because the continuous calculation of RS ensures that there will always be some average gain or average loss present. For example, find any chart where the currency pair has advanced for five consecutive bars and plot a five-period RSI. The RSI is not 100 although there is no average loss in the last five periods. The average gain ÷ average loss ratio (basic RS) is the basis for RSI. If RS is above 1, then RSI will be above 50 after RS is plugged into the calculation:

$$RSI = 100 - 100 \div (1 + RS)$$

If RS is below 1, then RSI will be below 50.

Many do not pay attention to the 50 line, but I find it useful. Much like rate of change above 0 or below 0 indicates a bullish or bearish bias, RSI above 50 or below 50 indicates a bullish or bearish bias. Wilder recommended labeling a market as overbought when RSI advanced above 70 and oversold when RSI fell below 30. When RSI is above 70, the idea is that the market in question has advanced too far too fast and that price is likely to at least pull back. While a traditional sell signal does not actually occur until RSI drops back below 70 (a traditional buy signal when RSI crosses above 30), I think that the indicator can be used more effectively.

Overbought and Oversold Is Erroneous

The concept of overbought and oversold in the traditional sense is flawed. Overbought and oversold could just as easily be termed strong uptrend and strong downtrend. Sure, price eventually reaches a peak or trough and turns, but not after remaining overbought or oversold for an extended period of time. The strongest trends (the ones that we as traders want to ride for as long as possible) can remain overbought or oversold, as the terms are defined in the traditional sense, for weeks or longer on daily charts.

Most novice traders will note that the RSI indicator is above 70; therefore, price is overbought and the correct decision is to sell. Oftentimes, the correct and therefore profitable decision is to do the exact opposite. The chart in Figure 6.19 is a weekly plot of the EURUSD. The bold bars indicate that 13-week RSI is below 30 or above 70. In nearly all of the instances, RSI moving above 70 was much closer to the beginning of a bull trend than to the end. Similarly, RSI moving below 30 was much closer to the beginning of a bear trend than to the end. Since the euro began trading in January 1999, there have been four instances when 13-week RSI crossed either above 70 or below 30. A change in the bias occurs only when RSI crosses into extreme territory in the opposite direction. For example, RSI crossed above 70 in May 2006 and since then has yet to cross below 30. Therefore, all the subsequent crosses above 70 are not counted as a cross

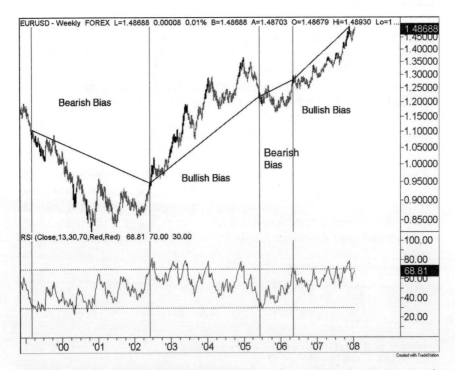

FIGURE 6.19 Overbought and oversold signal continuation of a trend more often than not. Using the indicator in this way would have helped you stay with much of the EURUSD bull market that began in 2000.
Source: Chart created on TradeStation®, the flagship product of TradeStation Technologies, Inc.

since the bias never changed from a long bias in the first place. The details are below.

- 13-week RSI crossed below 30 during the week that ended March 5, 1999. The EURUSD closed that week at 1.0818. The maximum drawdown would have been two weeks later at 1.1070. The maximum profit potential would have been in October 2000 when the EURUSD found bottom at .8227.
- 13-week RSI crossed above 70 during the week that ended June 7, 2002. The EURUSD closed that week at .9439. The maximum drawdown would have been the next week at .9387. The maximum profit potential would have been in December 2004 at 1.3666.
- 13-week RSI crossed below 30 during the week that ended June 10, 2005. The EURUSD closed that week at 1.2115. The maximum drawdown would have been in September 2006 at 1.2588. The maximum

profit potential would have been in November 2005 at 1.1638. This is the least profitable example.

- 13-week RSI crossed above 70 during the week that ended May 12, 2006. The EURUSD closed that week at 1.2920. The maximum drawdown would have been in July 2006 at 1.2458. The maximum profit potential would be 1.4967 to this point (this is December 2007). The bullish bias is still in place.

Figures 6.20 to 6.22 are examples of other currency pairs and time frames. As these charts indicate, RSI crossing 70 actually indicates with a high degree of probability that the bullish trend will extend. When the indicator crosses below 30, probability is high that the bearish trend will extend. If you prefer more timely signals, then change the RSI bullish barrier to 60 and the bearish barrier to 40 (see Figure 6.23). In this case, you

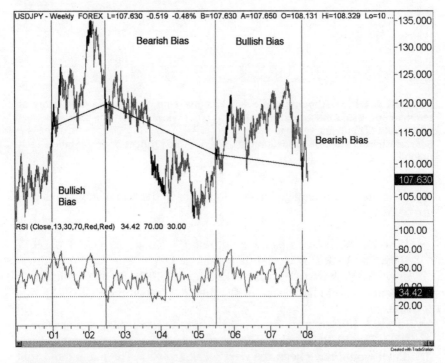

FIGURE 6.20 While the USDJPY results are not nearly as good as the EURUSD results, interpreting RSI in this manner would still have presented profitable opportunities
Source: Chart created on TradeStation®, the flagship product of TradeStation Technologies, Inc.

FIGURE 6.21 Interpreting RSI in this way can be applied on any time frame, as this example of the GBPUSD illustrates
Source: Chart created on TradeStation®, the flagship product of TradeStation Technologies, Inc.

would maintain a bullish bias following an RSI cross above 60 and a bearish bias following an RSI cross below 40.

As with any technical tool, RSI crosses above or below a specific level are not to be taken as blind signals. Rather, use the cross to determine a bias. For example, once RSI is above 60 on the weekly chart, buy intra-week weakness by placing orders near the calculated weekly pivot supports.

Stochastic Oscillator

The stochastic oscillator was developed by George Lane in 1959. At the time, the development of this indicator was revolutionary. Technical study of market action then was mostly confined to point and figure charting and Dow Theory, which is still applied to this day. Elliott wave theory was gaining publicity as well, thanks to Hamilton Bolton of the Bank Credit

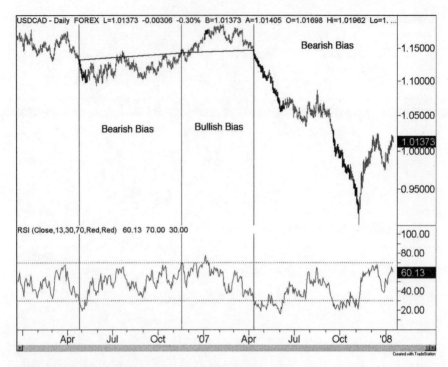

FIGURE 6.22 During very strong directional periods, interpreting RSI in this way keeps you from fading the trend as the USDCAD example shows
Source: Chart created on TradeStation®, the flagship product of TradeStation Technologies, Inc.

Analyst. Needless to say, Lane was a pioneer in the realm of oscillator analysis.

Lane actually studied Elliott wave theory himself and advocated using his stochastic indicator in conjunction with Elliott. What is interesting is the name that Lane chose for his indicator: stochastic. *Stochastic* means "randomness" and "unpredictability." Any practitioner of Elliott knows that markets are not random, but follow a basic form (which we will get to later). Probabilities can be predicted but are not certainties; in this way, one can make an argument that there is a certain degree of randomness but one cannot argue that markets are completely random. In any case, the name that Lane chose was stochastic.

The stochastic oscillator measures where the current closing price is, relative to the entire range over a specified amount of time. Like RSI, the oscillator is a limit oscillator with barriers of 100 and 0. The centerline would be 50. The logic behind the indicator is that the closing price in an

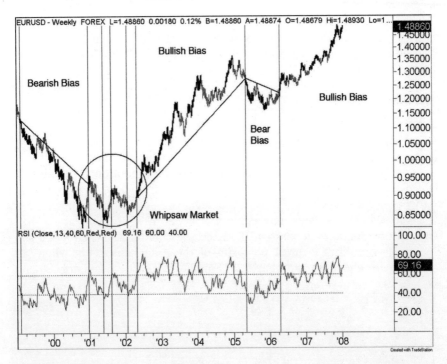

FIGURE 6.23 More timely signals can be achieved by using 60 and 40 instead of 70 and 30 for RSI. Of course, with more timely signals comes more false signals
Source: Chart created on TradeStation®, the flagship product of TradeStation Technologies, Inc.

uptrend will be closer to the top of the range over x number of periods and that the closing price will be closer to the low of the range over x number of periods. A reading of 100 indicates that the current closing price is the highest point of the range over x number of periods. A reading of 0 indicates that the current closing price is the lowest point of the range. Let's take a look at the calculation.

Fast Stochastics

%K = (current close − lowest low[n]) ÷ (highest high[n] − lowest low[n])

%D = a simple moving average of %K

n = number of periods specified

%K is the stochastic calculation and %D is just a moving average of %K. This version of the indicator is known as *fast stochastics*. Applying another moving average to %D yields *slow stochastics*. This is why the slow stochastic oscillator requires three inputs: one to specify the number of periods that determine the high-low range, one to determine the length of the first moving average, and one to determine the length of the second moving average.

Slow Stochastics

Fast %D becomes Slow %K

Slow %D = a simple moving average of Slow %K

As Figure 6.24 illustrates, slow stochastics is smooth and pleasing to the eye. Slow stochastics is more widely used, so from here on in this book, stochastic oscillator refers to slow stochastics.

Signals can be generated using crossovers. If %K crosses above %D, then a buy signal is generated. If %K crosses below %D, then a sell signal is generated. The most powerful of these signals occurs when %K and %D are above 80 and below 20. For the stochastic oscillator, 80 and

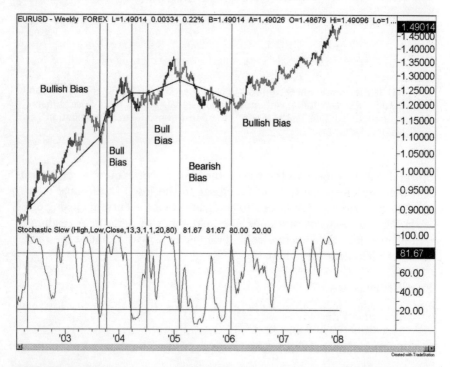

FIGURE 6.24 Slow stochastics looked at in the same way that RSI was before. Again, overbought and oversold often signal a continuation of the trend
Source: Chart created on TradeStation®, the flagship product of TradeStation Technologies, Inc.

20 designate overbought and oversold. One reason the stochastic oscillator is more sensitive an indicator than RSI, which is why the overbought and oversold levels are more extreme (80 and 20 for stochastic as opposed to 70 and 30 for RSI). Similar to RSI, the real reversal signal does not occur until the oscillator crosses back below 80 (for sell signals) and back above 20 (for buy signals).

Lane himself advocated using his indicator primarily to spot divergences in order to anticipate reversals (in conjunction with Elliott). As was mentioned previously, divergence does warn that the probability of the trend continuing is not as high as previous, but divergence can remain in place for a long time. The result is that traders try to sell the top or buy the bottom too early in almost all instances. When an oscillator is in extreme territory, take advantage of the trend by remaining with it instead of attempting to sell the top, which is what the majority of losing traders do.

The idea of maintaining a bullish bias as long as RSI has crossed above 60 and not yet crossed below 40 and maintaining a bearish bias as long as RSI has crossed below 40 but not yet crossed above 60 was a good one; the charts indicate that. Let's do the same thing with the stochastic oscillator. First, we will examine the EURUSD weekly chart with a 13, 3, 3 stochastic oscillator. We'll maintain a bullish bias as long as price has crossed above 80 without crossing below 20. We'll maintain a bearish bias as long as price has crossed below 20 without first crossing above 80.

The results are promising. If you compare Figure 6.24 to Figure 6.19, you'll notice that the stochastic oscillator signals the change in trend quicker than the RSI. The drawback though is that there are more false signals. RSI signals the first downtrend in the EURUSD in March 1999. The stochastic oscillator signals the downtrend two months earlier in January 1999. The RSI does not switch to a bullish bias until June 2002 but the stochastic oscillator gives a false buy signal in October 1999 before reverting back to a bearish bias the next month. From October 2000 until February 2002, the EURUSD traded in a range. With RSI, your bias would have remained bearish during this range bound period. With the stochastic oscillator, your bias would have changed multiple times. This is not necessarily a bad thing. The stochastic oscillator is more sensitive than RSI and therefore changes bias more often. This leads to earlier and timelier signals but also more false signals. Finding the correct balance between timeliness and reliability is essential to success in technical analysis. As is the case with any technical study of market action, this method of indentifying trend can be applied to any time frame, as the charts in Figures 6.25 to 6.27 demonstrate.

If you wish to make the stochastic oscillator trend signal even timelier, then change the point at which you adopt a bullish bias from 80 to 70 and a bearish bias from 20 to 30, as shown in Figure 6.28.

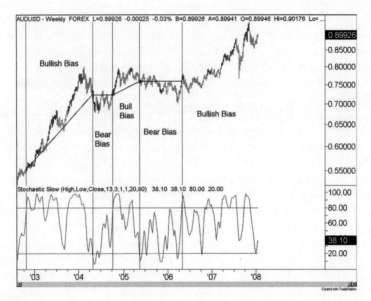

FIGURE 6.25 The method works well with the weekly AUDUSD chart. Even false signals end up as flat trades at worst
Source: Chart created on TradeStation®, the flagship product of TradeStation Technologies, Inc.

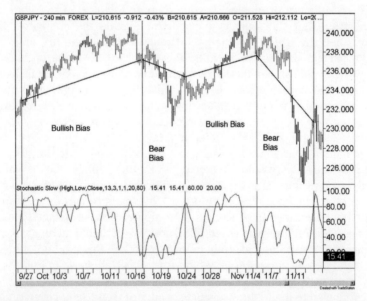

FIGURE 6.26 Using this method with GBPJPY on this 240-minute chart helps catch the big swings that the pair is infamous for
Source: Chart created on TradeStation®, the flagship product of TradeStation Technologies, Inc.

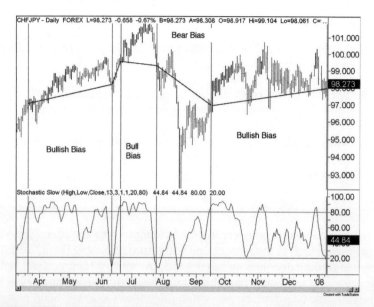

FIGURE 6.27 Interpreting slow stochastics this way on the CHFJPY daily chart helps in catching both up and down moves
Source: Chart created on TradeStation®, the flagship product of TradeStation Technologies, Inc.

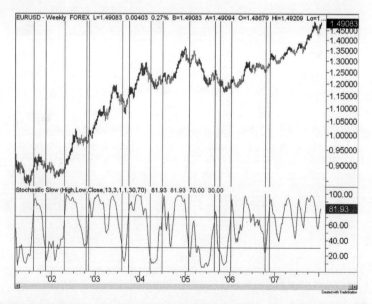

FIGURE 6.28 Changing the parameters from 80, 20 to 70, 30 results in timelier but more false signals. The stochastic oscillator is more volatile than RSI
Source: Chart created on TradeStation®, the flagship product of TradeStation Technologies, Inc.

Bollinger Bands

John Bollinger developed Bollinger bands in the early 1980s. The following is an excerpt from bollingerbands.com:

> *The purpose of Bollinger Bands is to provide a relative definition of high and low. By definition prices are high at the upper band and low at the lower band.*
>
> *Middle Bollinger Band = 20-period simple moving average*
>
> *Upper Bollinger Band = Middle Bollinger Band + 2 * 20-period standard deviation*
>
> *Lower Bollinger Band = Middle Bollinger Band − 2 * 20-period standard deviation*

The first few sentences can be misleading to a new trader. "By definition prices are high at the upper band and low at the lower band." Although success in trading depends on buying at a lower price than you sell, selling when price is at the upper band based on the assumption that price is high can be ruinous. Likewise, buying when price is at the lower band based on the idea that price is low usually results in fading a downtrend. In range bound markets, Bollinger bands work like a charm at identifying the top and bottom of the range as illustrated in Figure 6.29.

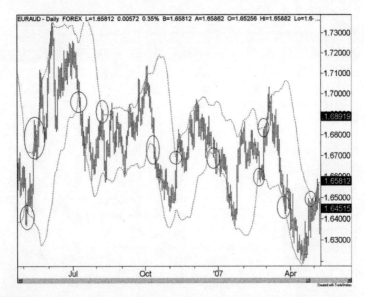

FIGURE 6.29   Bollinger band gauge support and resistance well in range bound markets
Source: Chart created on TradeStation®, the flagship product of TradeStation Technologies, Inc.

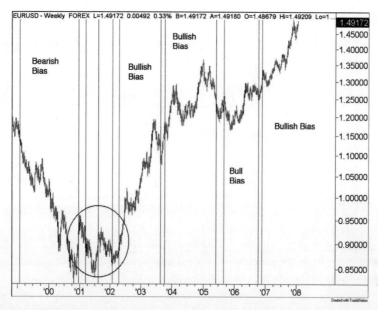

FIGURE 6.30 The bold bars indicate when price closes above the 2 standard deviation upper Bollinger band or below the 2 standard deviation lower Bollinger band
Source: Chart created on TradeStation®, the flagship product of TradeStation Technologies, Inc.

I still contend that the big money is to be made in trending markets. Continually buying near the bottom of the band and selling near the top of the band will cause you to miss out on the best money-making opportunities that the market presents. You can probably guess by now where I am going with this. It is more profitable to adopt a bullish bias when price exceeds the upper band and a bearish bias when price drops below the lower band, as illustrated in Figure 6.30.

Buying strength and selling weakness based on price exceeding the upper band and dropping below the lower band is the same as buying when RSI or the stochastic oscillator indicate that price is overbought or oversold. If you prefer a timelier signal from the Bollinger bands, then change the standard deviation setting from 2 to 1, as illustrated in Figure 6.31.

Using these indicators in the way that I have presented them is much more useful than the traditional approach. To prove that point, I ran very basic tests on the EURUSD weekly chart. The following rules apply:

- Once the bias changes from short to long, a stop buy order is placed to buy at the high.
- Once the bias changes from long to short, a stop sell order is placed to sell short at the low.

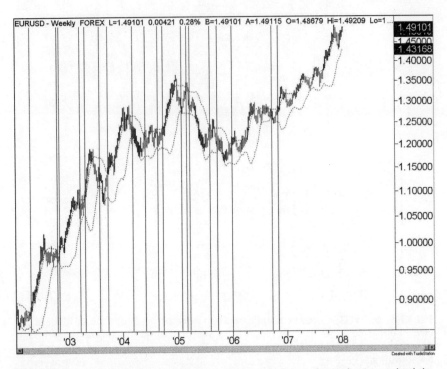

FIGURE 6.31 The bold bars indicate when price closes above the 1 standard deviation upper Bollinger band or below the 1 standard deviation lower Bollinger band
Source: Chart created on TradeStation®, the flagship product of TradeStation Technologies, Inc.

The bias is determined as presented in this chapter. The tests were for RSI(70, 30), RSI(60, 40), stochastic oscillator(80, 20), stochastic oscillator(70, 30), Bollinger band(2 stdev), and Bollinger band(1 stdev). I ran three more tests: one each for RSI, the stochastic oscillator, and Bollinger bands, to illustrate that using them to trade reversals does not work so well. For RSI and the stochastic oscillator, the rules are to sell at the low of the bar once the indicator crosses below the overbought level (70 for RSI and 80 for the stochastic oscillator). Similarly, a buy order is placed at the high of the bar once the indicator crosses above the oversold level (30 and 20). I used 13 as the length for both oscillators. The Bollinger band reversal strategy sells at the low of the bar once the price crosses and closes below the upper band. A buy order is placed at the high of the bar when the price crosses and closes above the lower band. I used a 21-week lookback period and bands of 1 and 2 standard deviations. There are equity curves for nine strategies (2 each for the RSI, stochastics, and Bollinger band trend

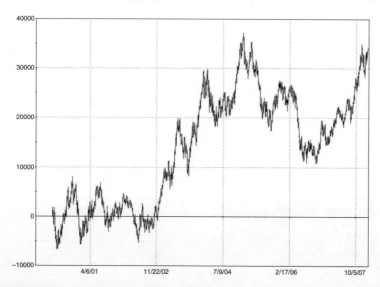

FIGURE 6.32 RSI (70, 30) trending strategy
Source: Chart created on TradeStation®, the flagship product of TradeStation Technologies, Inc.

strategies and 1 each for the RSI, stochastics, and Bollinger band reversal strategies). See Figures 6.32 to 6.40.

The results speak for themselves. Does this mean that you recklessly buy and sell when an indicator crosses a certain threshold? Of course not; other variables such as the market's pattern and overall structure (see Chapter 7) must be considered. This is not a strategy in itself, but the objective of the tests is to show that determining a bullish or bearish bias in the way that I have presented can serve as the foundation for a successful trading strategy.

WHEN TO GET OUT

This chapter concentrated on determining a bias, but what about exiting the position? Waiting for the bias to change from bullish to bearish to exit our bullish position will result in too large a loss of paper profits. Even though determining a bias can be approached systematically, determining when you are no longer justified in holding the position requires more skill, in my opinion. In this sense, determining when to exit is more art than science.

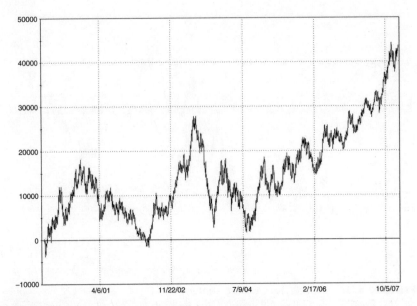

FIGURE 6.33 Slow stochastics (80, 20) trending strategy
Source: Chart created on TradeStation®, the flagship product of TradeStation Technologies, Inc.

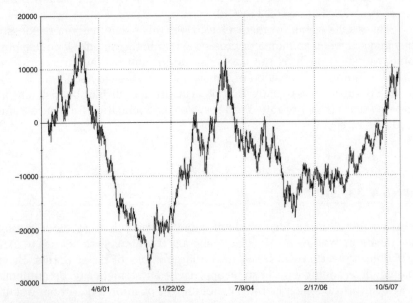

FIGURE 6.34 Bollinger band 2 standard deviation trending strategy
Source: Chart created on TradeStation®, the flagship product of TradeStation Technologies, Inc.

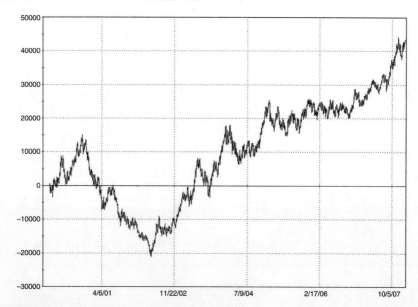

FIGURE 6.35   RSI (60, 40) trending strategy
Source: Chart created on TradeStation®, the flagship product of TradeStation Technologies, Inc.

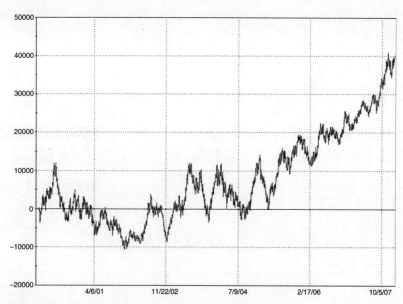

FIGURE 6.36   Slow stochastics (70, 30) trending strategy
Source: Chart created on TradeStation®, the flagship product of TradeStation Technologies, Inc.

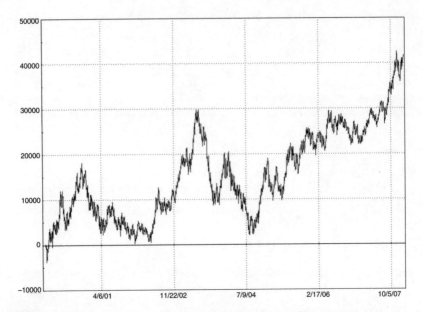

FIGURE 6.37 Bollinger band 1 standard deviation trending strategy
Source: Chart created on TradeStation®, the flagship product of TradeStation Technologies, Inc.

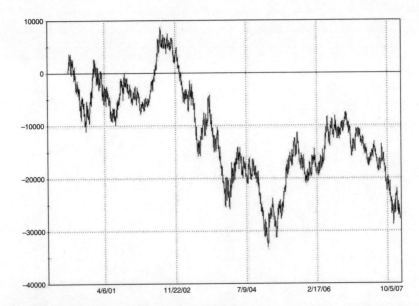

FIGURE 6.38 RSI (70, 30) reversal strategy
Source: Chart created on TradeStation®, the flagship product of TradeStation Technologies, Inc.

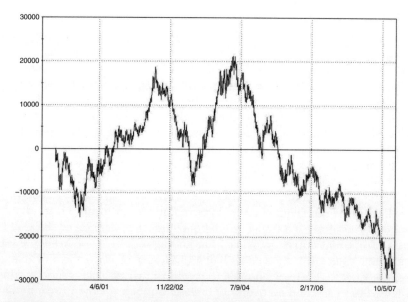

FIGURE 6.39 Slow stochastics (80, 20) reversal strategy
Source: Chart created on TradeStation®, the flagship product of TradeStation Technologies, Inc.

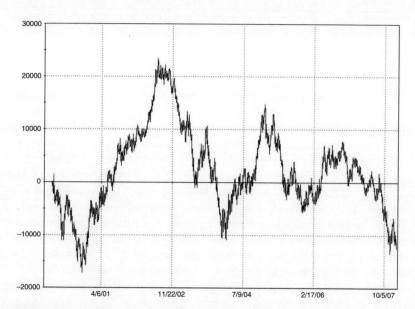

FIGURE 6.40 Bollinger band 2 standard deviation reversal strategy
Source: Chart created on TradeStation®, the flagship product of TradeStation Technologies, Inc.

Consecutive Up and Down Periods

Much like a rate of change extreme announces the start of a new trend, a consecutive number of closes in the same direction often announces that the trend is reaching a point of exhaustion. A currency pair that closes up or down for x number of periods in a row indicates near complete agreement among market participants as to the direction of the market. The market could be crowded with too many bulls (in the case of consecutive up periods) or too many bears (in the case of consecutive down periods). An analogy that accurately describes the state of the market during this time is that of a boat with too many people sitting on one side. What happens? The boat tips over. The same thing happens in financial markets and in the FX market in particular.

Fear is the dominant emotion in the FX market. Currencies are traded in pairs. Therefore, if a trader is long one currency, then he or she is also short a different currency. What I am getting at is that a currency is often bought since it is viewed as being the lesser of two evils. For example, the EURUSD rate has not skyrocketed to record levels recently (this is late 2007) based on an overly optimistic outlook for the Eurozone but rather because of fear of the U.S. dollar. Fear is an extremely powerful emotion, much more so than hope or greed. Fear leads to panic, and panic is reflected through price as strings of consecutive up and down days (or weeks, etc.). When fear is the greatest, the currency in question will find a bottom and begin to rally. In the case of the EURUSD, fear toward the U.S. dollar registers a peak at the top of the chart. Fear toward the euro would register its extreme at the bottom of the chart. Figures 6.41 to 6.44 are examples of tops and bottoms that formed following a number of consecutive closes in the same direction.

I have showed weekly charts in order to show major tops and bottoms that can occur following a string of consecutive closes in the same direction. However, this dynamic can be applied to daily charts and even smaller time frames, even though the turns will not be as significant.

By no means should you wait for a consecutive number of up or down closes to close your position. Rather, if you are fortunate enough to exit your position following one of these instances, then take advantage of the situation and do so. The best time to exit the trend is at the sentiment extreme (a bullish sentiment extreme if you are long and a bearish sentiment extreme if you are short), and consecutive closes in one direction represent a sentiment extreme. Use 8 as a starting point. For example, once a pair has rallied for 8 weeks (or days), place a stop just below the low of the last week (week 8 if this is week 9). If week 9 ends up, then move the stop to the low of week 9 for week 10. Repeat this process until you are stopped out.

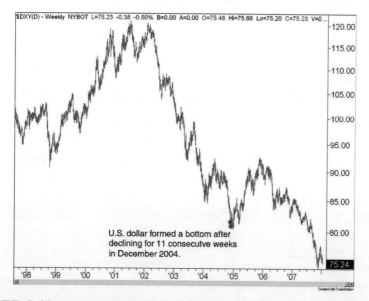

FIGURE 6.41 Dollar Index weekly bars: The USD formed a bottom after declining for 11 consecutive weeks in December 2004
Source: Chart created on TradeStation®, the flagship product of TradeStation Technologies, Inc.

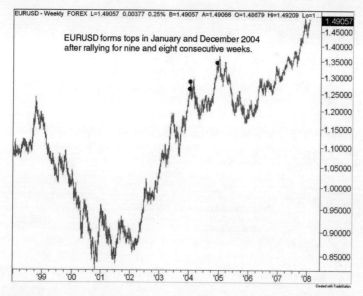

FIGURE 6.42 EURUSD weekly bars: The EURUSD formed tops in January and December 2004 after rallying for 9 and 8 consecutive weeks
Source: Chart created on TradeStation®, the flagship product of TradeStation Technologies, Inc.

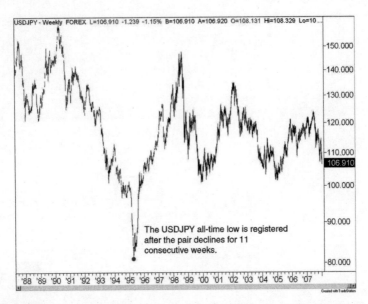

FIGURE 6.43 USDJPY weekly bars: The USDJPY all-time low occurred after the pair declined for 11 consecutive weeks in 1995
Source: Chart created on TradeStation®, the flagship product of TradeStation Technologies, Inc.

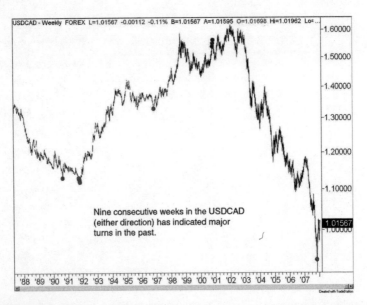

FIGURE 6.44 USDCAD weekly bars: Major turns in the USDCAD tend to occur after moves of nine consecutive weeks
Source: Chart created on TradeStation®, the flagship product of TradeStation Technologies, Inc.

Theoretically, if the best exit is at a sentiment extreme, then the best entry should also be at the sentiment extreme. Of course, this often results in trying to be too perfect. To combat trying to be too perfect, determine the bias systematically in the way that I described in this chapter. You may not actually get into the trend until just before the midpoint, but you will catch the bulk of the move and the blow-off top that occurs so often in FX. I believe that this is a strong methodology.

CHAPTER 7

Explanation of Elliott Wave and Fibonacci

I n this chapter, I will cover the basic rules, of which there are just a few, of wave formation and introduce setups for timing your trade. "A rule is so called because it governs all waves to which it applies. Characteristics of waves are called guidelines."[1] Many guidelines of impulse formation and many details pertaining to corrective patterns are not covered here. Also covered briefly in this chapter is Fibonacci analysis. Many traders are familiar with Fibonacci retracements but do not realize that Fibonacci was first introduced as a method of technical analysis by R. N. Elliott. In fact, Fibonacci is the mathematical basis for the wave principle.

If you long for a fuller understanding of Elliott (which includes Fibonacci), then I urge you to read the books listed in the Notes section at the back of the book. An experienced Elliottician has at his or her disposal what I believe to be one of the most powerful market timing tools in existence.

WHO WAS ELLIOTT?

Ralph Nelson Elliott was a successful accountant early in the twentieth century and "held executive positions primarily with railroad companies in Mexico and Central America." His success in turning around troubled rail companies attracted the attention of the U.S. State Department, and in 1924 the department "chose him to become the Chief Accountant for Nicaragua, which was under the control of the U.S. marines at the time."

Elliott moved to Guatemala City after the United States extricated itself from Nicaragua to take on the position of general auditor of the International Railway of Central America. While in Central America in the late 1920s, Elliott contracted an "alimentary tract illness caused by the organism amoeba histolytica."[2]

At 58 years of age, the former accountant was very sick and confined to his home. His mind always at work (he had written two books), Elliott dedicated his time to studying the price behavior of the Dow Jones Averages. Elliott studied many time frames, from 30 minute to yearly. This must have been quite an arduous task given that charts were plotted by hand on graph paper then.

Elliott discovered that price action displayed on different time frames formed the same basic patterns. In other words, there is a market form at all degrees of trend. The basic pattern that Elliott discovered was that a market cycle consists of eight waves, five waves with the trend and three waves against the trend. Within the five waves, waves 1, 3, and 5 are in the direction of the trend while waves 2 and 4 are against the trend, or corrections of the trend. Wave 2 corrects wave 1 and wave 4 corrects wave 3. Following the completion of five waves in one direction, a larger correction takes place in three waves. The basic 5–3 pattern forms the foundation from which everything else is a part. Figure 7.1 shows the basic pattern of five waves with the trend and three waves against the trend.

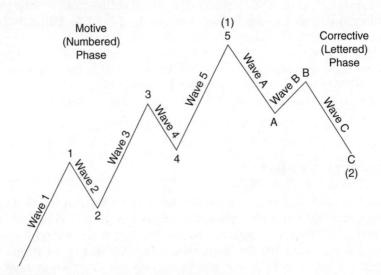

FIGURE 7.1 Basic Five Wave Idealized Pattern
Source: Courtesy of Elliott Wave International, Inc.

Fractal Nature of Markets

Elliott discovered that price action exhibited the same basic patterns regardless of time frame. The patterns come together to form similar but larger patterns. For example, the patterns on the 30-minute chart link together to form similar patterns on the daily chart, which link together to form similar patterns on a monthly chart. This idea, that the patterns are the same regardless of time frame, would come to be known as fractal. The term *fractal* was actually coined by Benoit Mandelbrot in 1975 and is described by him as "a rough or fragmented geometric shape that can be subdivided in parts, each of which is (at least approximately) a reduced-size copy of the whole."[3] The word is derived from the Latin *fractus* meaning "broken" or "fractured." Although termed by Mandelbrot, Elliott had discovered almost 50 years earlier that financial markets are fractal in nature. In this sense, the wave principle is not just a trading and forecasting tool but also a "detailed description of how markets behave"[4] The fractal nature of markets is illustrated in Figure 7.2.

Elliott also found the same recurring patterns on the charts regardless of the market that he was studying. If different markets are supposed to react to different news stories and events, then why would the different markets exhibit the same patterns? The only answer is that freely traded financial markets are not influenced by outside forces but are instead

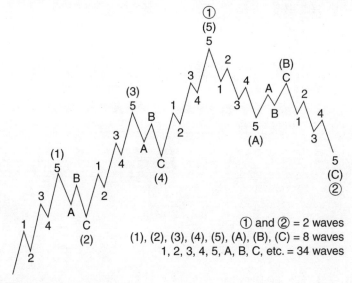

① and ② = 2 waves
(1), (2), (3), (4), (5), (A), (B), (C) = 8 waves
1, 2, 3, 4, 5, A, B, C, etc. = 34 waves

FIGURE 7.2 Market Design
Source: Courtesy of Elliott Wave International, Inc.

endogenous. In other words, markets have a life of their own. That life is collective psychology or crowd behavior, which oscillates between pessimism and optimism in a patterned way. Elliott wave analysis can be applied to stocks, commodities, currencies, real estate, metals, energy, or any other freely traded market. The only requirement is that the market be freely traded. Without a freely traded market, the expression of crowd behavior as seen through the waves is not visible. Figures 7.3 to 7.5 are examples of different markets and different time frames, but the basic 5–3 pattern is visible regardless.

Motive Waves

Motive waves move in the direction of the larger trend. Waves 1, 3, and 5 are motive waves. Each motive wave consists of five waves. The idealized version of a motive wave is shown in Figure 7.6. "Within motive waves, wave 2 always retraces less than 100 percent of wave 1, and wave 4 always

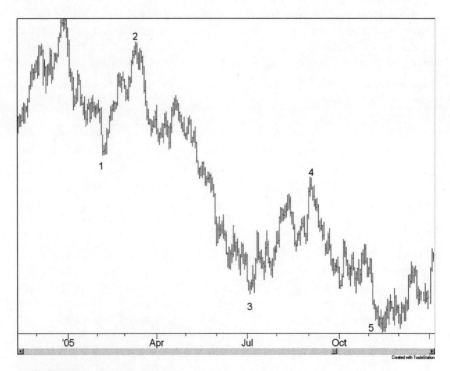

FIGURE 7.3   EURUSD Daily Bars
Source: Chart created on TradeStation®, the flagship product of TradeStation Technologies, Inc.

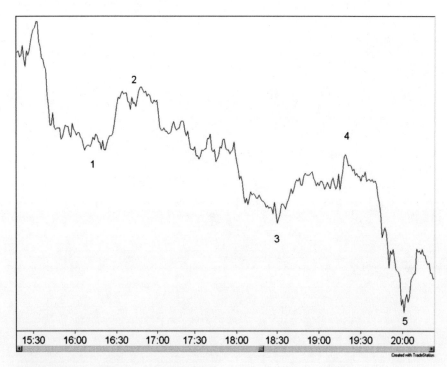

FIGURE 7.4 USDJPY One-Minute Bars
Source: Chart created on TradeStation®, the flagship product of TradeStation Technologies, Inc.

retraces less than 100 percent of wave 3. Wave 3, moreover, always travels beyond the end of wave 1. The goal of a motive wave is to make progress, and these rules assure that it will."[5] Wave 3 is never the shortest wave and often the longest, according to Elliott himself. In currencies though, I have noticed many times that wave 5 is the longest.

Impulse Waves A motive wave is either an impulse or a diagonal. The examples so far in this chapter depict impulse waves. In an impulse wave, wave 4 does not overlap with any of wave 1. As the impulse itself consists of five waves, waves 1, 3, and 5 of the impulse are also motive waves, and wave 3 of the impulse is an impulse. The strong, nearly vertical movements that you see on a chart are impulse waves. Examples of impulse waves are shown in Figures 7.7 to 7.9.

Diagonals Diagonals occur at either the very beginning of a trend in wave 1 (rare), or at the end of a very strong trend in wave 5. Elliott

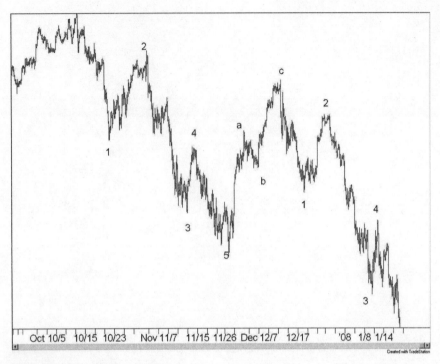

FIGURE 7.5   Dow Hourly Bars
Source: Chart created on TradeStation®, the flagship product of TradeStation Technologies, Inc.

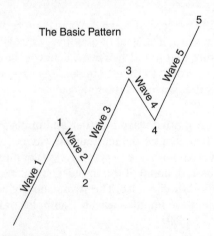

FIGURE 7.6   Idealized Motive
Source: Courtesy of Elliott Wave International, Inc.

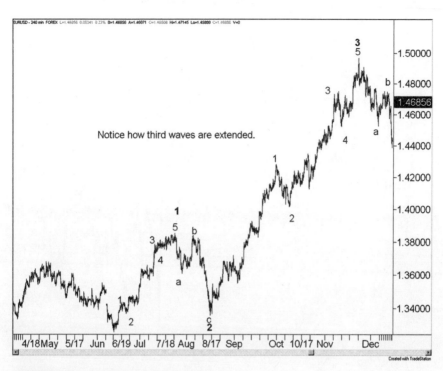

FIGURE 7.7 EURUSD 240-Minute Bars
Source: Chart created on TradeStation®, the flagship product of TradeStation Technologies, Inc.

described diagonals as occurring when "the preceding trend has gone too far too fast."[6] In a diagonal, wave 4 often does overlap wave 1 although this is not a requirement. Whereas a diagonal does consist of five waves and wave 3 cannot be the shortest wave, each of the five waves consists of three waves. The most common type of diagonal is a contracting one, in which two lines converge, like a diagonal triangle. The name *diagonal* originated from this tendency. The other type of diagonal that Elliott wrote about was an expanding diagonal; which is extremely rare. The pattern that forms from the price action (see Figures 7.10, 7.11, and 7.12) is a reflection of collective market psychology.

With this in mind, think about why an expanding triangle is rare. Diagonal or not, triangles reflect a balance of bullish and bearish forces that creates a low volatility environment. In contrast, volatility increases in an expanding triangle or diagonal. It is rare indeed for volatility to increase despite a sideways trend (which brings up the point that trend does have three classifications: up, down, and sideways). Chart patterns indicate

FIGURE 7.8   USDJPY 240-Minute Bars
Source: Chart created on TradeStation®, the flagship product of TradeStation Technologies, Inc.

more about the psychological state of the market than novices originally recognize.

Zigzag

A zigzag correction is a sharp correction that is labeled A–B–C. In a bull market (waves 1, 3, and 5 are advancing waves), wave A of the zigzag is a five wave decline, wave B of the zigzag is a three wave rally, and wave C of the zigzag is a five wave decline. Zigzags are most commonly seen in wave 2 of a five wave impulse.

In a zigzag, the initial five wave decline (wave A) makes it difficult for wave B to retrace a significant portion of wave A. In other words, wave B within a correction is often shallow, retracing roughly 38.2 to 50 percent of wave A before wave C begins. Wave C is often similar to wave A. In fact, wave C is the same as wave A with regard to form; both waves A and C are five wave impulses. In terms of price distance, waves A and C tend toward

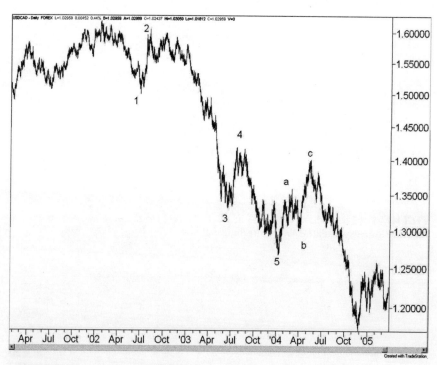

FIGURE 7.9 USDCAD Daily Bars
Source: Chart created on TradeStation®, the flagship product of TradeStation Technologies, Inc.

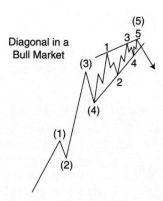

FIGURE 7.10 Idealized Diagonal in a Bull Market from *Elliott Wave Principle*
Source: Courtesy of Elliott Wave International, Inc.

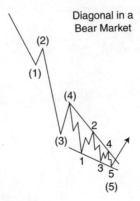

FIGURE 7.11 Idealized Diagonal in a Bear Market from *Elliott Wave Principle*
Source: Courtesy of Elliott Wave International, Inc.

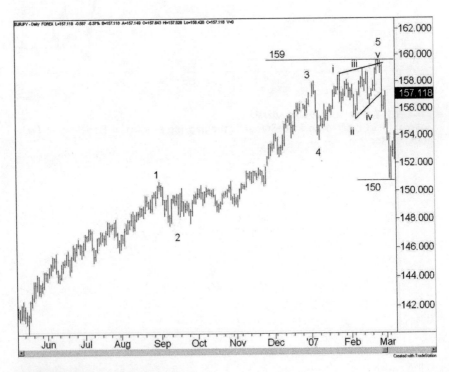

FIGURE 7.12 EURJPY Daily Bars
Source: Chart created on TradeStation®, the flagship product of TradeStation Technologies, Inc.

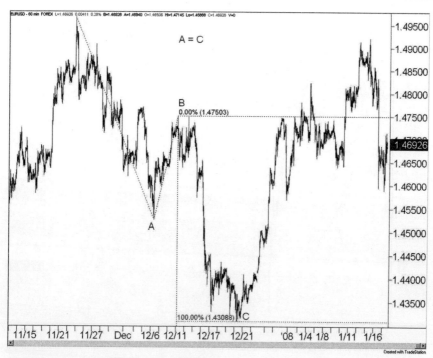

FIGURE 7.13 EURUSD 60-Minute Bars
Source: Chart created on TradeStation®, the flagship product of TradeStation Technologies, Inc.

equality. Sometimes, waves A and C are related by the Fibonacci ratio (.618 or 1.618). Figures 7.13 and 7.14 show instances when waves A and C tend toward equality in terms of price distance (in pips).

Flat

A flat is a more shallow correction, hence the name *flat.* Just like a zigzag, a flat is labeled A–B–C, but the form of a flat differs from that of a zigzag. In a bull market, wave A of a flat is a three wave decline, wave B of a flat is a three wave rally, and wave C of a flat is a five wave decline. Flats are commonly seen in the wave 4 position.

Contrary to a zigzag, wave A in a flat is not sharp. Therefore, wave B often retraces at least 61.8 percent of wave A. It is not uncommon for wave B to actually exceed the origin of wave A. When this happens, the pattern unfolding is called an expanded flat. Wave C, in five waves, does the most correcting and almost always ends below the end of wave A. When wave

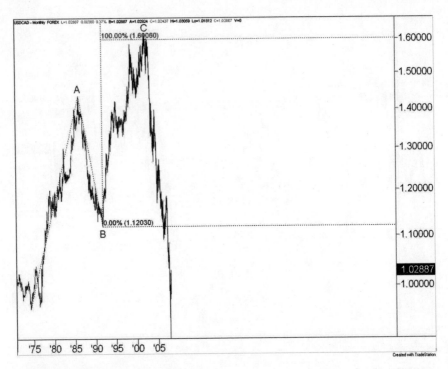

FIGURE 7.14 USDCAD Monthly Bars
Source: Chart created on TradeStation®, the flagship product of TradeStation Technologies, Inc.

C fails to end below wave A, the pattern is called a *running flat.* A regular flat can be seen in Figure 7.15 and an expanded flat in Figure 7.16.

Triangles

Triangles are everywhere and occur commonly as wave 4 within a five wave impulse or wave B within a three wave correction. As previously mentioned, triangles reflect a balance of forces and usually result in a low volatility environment (unless they are expanding triangles). Triangles usually unfold in five waves, labeled A–B–C–D–E.

Alternating legs of the triangle are often related by .618. For example, the price distance of wave C is 61.8 percent of the price distance of wave A. Wave D is 61.8 percent of the price distance of wave B and wave E is 61.8 percent of the price distance of wave C. Not every single alternating leg will tend toward this relationship. In reality, probably just one

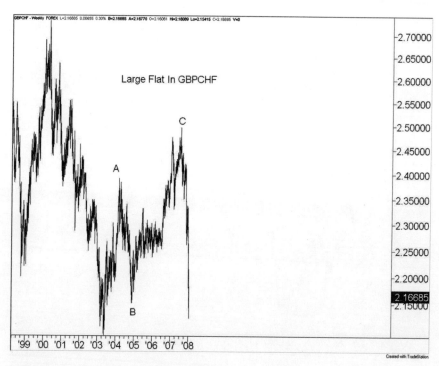

GBPCHF - Weekly FOREX L=2.16685 0.00695 0.30% B=2.16685 A=2.16770 O=2.16061 Hi=2.18089 Lo=2.15415 C=2.16685 V=0

Large Flat In GBPCHF

FIGURE 7.15 GBPCHF Weekly Bars
Source: Chart created on TradeStation®, the flagship product of TradeStation Technologies, Inc.

set of alternating legs within a triangle will exhibit this relationship. Form is always most important. Examples of triangles are shown in Figures 7.17 and 7.18.

FIBONACCI: THE MATHEMATICAL FOUNDATION

The mathematical basis for the wave principle is the Fibonacci sequence. Leonardo Fibonacci of Pisa published *Liber Abacci* (Book of Calculation) in the early 1200s and introduced the decimal system to Europe in the process. Fibonacci's introduction of what became known as the Hindu-Arabic system laid the foundation for advancements in higher mathematics, physics, astronomy, and engineering.

FIGURE 7.16 EURJPY Daily Bars
Source: Chart created on TradeStation®, the flagship product of TradeStation Technologies, Inc.

In *Liber Abacci*, the famous rabbit problem is posed:

> *How many pairs of rabbits placed in an enclosed area can be produced in a single year from one pair of rabbits if each pair gives birth to a new pair each month starting with the second month?*
>
> *"In arriving at the solution, we find that each pair, including the first pair, needs a month's time to mature, but once in production, begets a new pair each month. The number of pairs is the same at the beginning of each of the first two months, so the sequence is 1, 1. The first pair finally doubles its number during the second month, so that there are two pairs at the beginning of the third month. Of these, the older pair begets a third pair the following month so that at the beginning of the fourth month, the sequence expands 1, 1, 2, 3. Of these three, the two older pairs reproduce, but not the youngest pair, so the number of rabbit pairs expands to five. The next month, three pairs reproduce so the sequence expands to 1, 1, 2, 3, 5, 8 and so forth."*[7]

USDJPY - Weekly FOREX L=107.104 -0.516 -0.48% B=107.104 A=107.129 O=107.585 H=107.878 Lo=106.806 C=107.104 V=0

12-Year Triangle in USDJPY

FIGURE 7.17 USDJPY Weekly Bars
Source: Chart created on TradeStation®, the flagship product of TradeStation Technologies, Inc.

The family grows exponentially and the sequence that results is known as the Fibonacci sequence, which "has many interesting properties and reflects an almost constant relationship among its components."[8]

Summing any two adjacent numbers yields the next number in the sequence: 1, 1, 2, 3, 5, 8, 13, 21, 34, 55, 89, 144, and so forth. Dividing a number in the sequence by its preceding number is approximately 1.618 and by its next number is .618. The farther down the sequence, the closer the ratio is to the irrational number phi, .618034. Dividing alternate numbers yields .382 (.382 + .618 = 1) and the inverse of .382 is 2.618. A table of ratios is shown in Figure 7.19.

Fibonacci numbers and ratios derived from Fibonacci numbers are found everywhere. Music is based on the eight-note octave. A piano has eight white keys and five black keys for a total of 13. The most pleasant sound to the human ear is the major sixth. The ratio of vibration between notes E and C is .625, just thousandths from phi (.618034). "William Hoffer, writing for the December 1975 *Smithsonian Magazine*, wrote: '...the

FIGURE 7.18   EURCHF 60-Minute Bars
Source: Chart created on TradeStation®, the flagship product of TradeStation Technologies, Inc.

proportion of .618034 to 1 is the mathematical basis for the shape of playing cards and the Parthenon, sunflowers and snail shells, Greek vases and the spiral galaxies of outer space. The Greeks based much of their art and architecture upon this proportion.'"[9]

The golden ratio can be found in the microtubules of the brain, DNA molecules, planetary orbits, and galaxies. In the sixteenth century, Johannes Kepler said that the golden ratio "described virtually all of creation and specifically symbolized God's creation of 'like from like.'"[10] Even humans are divided into Fibonacci proportion. The average distance from the navel to the top of the head divided by the distance from the navel down to the bottom of the feet is .618.

The point is that if Fibonacci numbers and the ratios derived from them are found throughout life, then it makes sense that these same numbers and ratios would be found in activities that encompass large masses of humans; such as markets. Figure 7.20 illustrates how a market's form is determined by Fibonacci numbers.

Fibonacci Ratio Table

NUMERATOR → DENOMINATOR ↓	1	2	3	5	8	13	21	34	55	89	144
1	1.00	2.00	3.00	5.00	8.00	13.00	21.00	34.00	55.00	89.00	144.00
2	.50	1.00	1.50	2.50	4.00	6.50	10.50	17.00	27.50	44.50	72.00
3	.333	.667	1.00	1.667	2.667	4.33	7.00	11.33	18.33	29.67	48.00
5	.20	.40	.60	1.00	1.60	2.60	4.20	6.80	11.00	17.80	28.80
8	.125	.25	.375	.625	1.00	1.625	2.625	4.25	6.875	11.125	18.00
13	.077	.154	.231	.385	.615	1.00	1.615	2.615	4.23	6.846	11.077
21	.0476	.0952	.1429	.238	.381	.619	1.00	1.619	2.619	4.238	6.857
34	.0294	.0588	.0882	.147	.235	.3824	.6176	1.00	1.618	2.618	4.235
55	.01818	.03636	.0545	.0909	.1455	.236	.3818	.618	1.00	1.618	2.618
89	.011236	.02247	.0337	.05618	.08989	.146	.236	.382	.618	1.00	1.618
144	.006944	.013889	.0208	.0347	.05556	.0903	.1458	.236	.382	.618	1.00

Towards perfect ratios

FIGURE 7.19 Fibonacci Ratio Table
Source: Courtesy of Elliott Wave International, Inc.

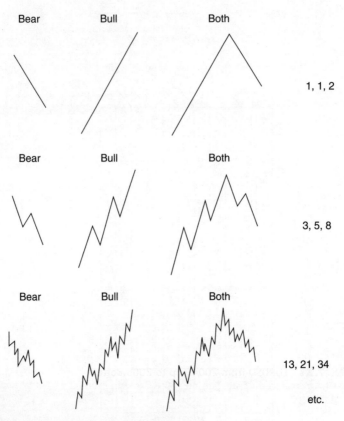

FIGURE 7.20 Fibonacci in Market Form
Source: Courtesy of Elliott Wave International, Inc.

RATIOS

This is a brief list of relationships that are found among waves. By no means are these relationships always found, but they are often found. Form is the most important aspect to consider when applying wave analysis, but ratios help pinpoint entry and exit levels as well. Remember that wave 3 is never the shortest. These relationships below assume that wave 3 is extended. The legs of the EURUSD decline from December 2004 to November 2005 exhibited the relationships listed below. See Figure 7.21 for a visual representation of the decline.

Wave 2 = .618 to .786 of wave 1
Wave 3 = 1.618 of wave 1

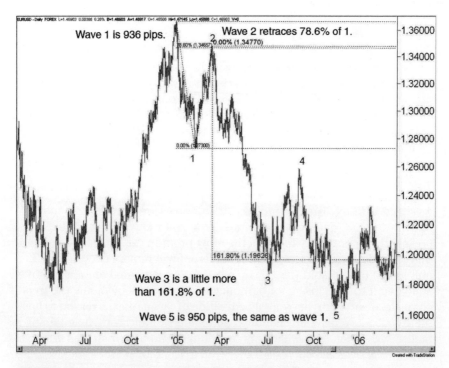

FIGURE 7.21 EURUSD from 2004 Top to 2005 Bottom
Source: Chart created on TradeStation®, the flagship product of TradeStation Technologies, Inc.

Wave 4 = .236 to .382 of wave 3

Wave 5 = Wave 1

Wave B = .618 to 1.382 of wave A

Wave C = 1 to 1.618 of wave C

SPECIFIC SETUPS

One of the knocks on Elliott wave analysis is that counts change, which makes trading with Elliott difficult. For example, a trader might go short, expecting a wave 4 correction to end near the 38.2 percent retrace level of wave 3. A triangle unfolds instead and gives way to the wave 5 advance before price reaches the 38.2 percent Fibonacci level. The trader's stop is triggered, and the result is a losing trade. This hypothetical example highlights one of the most common barriers to success: overtrading. Not every single price movement should be traded. In fact, most price movements should *not* be traded.

I believe there are four instances in the wave structure when the probability of success and the reward-to-risk ratio warrant taking action, even if that action would be considered to be fading the existing trend. There are concrete rules and specific patterns to look for. In these instances, fading the trend is intelligent, not reckless. The setups are listed below in order of their profit potential.

1–2 Base

As stated in *Elliott Wave Principle*, "Third waves are wonders to behold."[11] Third waves are quite often the most powerful motive wave (1, 3, 5) and present the opportunity to catch the most profit in the shortest amount of time. It is during third waves that oscillators will remain overbought (in a bull trend) or oversold (in a bear trend) for an extended amount of time. Many retail traders lose a lot of money in third waves by fading the trend, citing the overbought or oversold condition of the market as reason to buck the trend. As we saw in Chapter 6 on technical indicators, maintaining a bullish bias when an oscillator is overbought and a bearish bias when an oscillator is oversold serves a trader well in trending periods such as third waves.

Once a five wave impulse is identified, look to enter in the direction of that impulse following a correction. In other words, a five wave rally will give way to a three wave decline. It is the three wave decline that presents the high probability bullish opportunity. If the five wave impulse occurs from a significant low or high, then the reward-to-risk ratio will be greatest (significant as it pertains to the high or low that is traded against is relative, of course). A trader that typically holds positions for a month probably regards a six-month high as significant while a trader that holds positions for one day regards a two-week high as significant. Regardless, a five wave impulse can be seen on a daily chart, a five-minute chart, and all other time frames.

As mentioned, look to enter in the direction of the impulse following a correction. Form is always the overriding determinant in Elliott but a correction that follows an impulse rally (or decline) from a significant low (or high) will usually retrace at least 50 percent of the preceding impulse, and often end near the 61.8 percent level. Additionally, an impulse from a significant high or low is either the first wave in a new five wave bull or bear cycle (1–2–3–4–5) or the first wave in a new three wave bull or bear cycle (A–B–C). Knowing where you are in the larger degree wave structure is extremely important at all times. So, you should have an idea whether or not the initial five wave impulse is wave 1 or wave A of a zigzag. In any case, a stop can be placed just below the low (or high) of what at this point is either the origin of wave 1 or wave A of a zigzag. I initially enter with just one-half of my full position. I place an order to enter the rest of the position above the top of what is either wave 1 or wave A (bottom of wave 1 or wave A if the impulse was down A). I prefer to enter small initially because nothing is foolproof. I believe that probability is high enough that entering a small position on the pullback is warranted but wave 3 (or wave C of the zigzag) is not confirmed until price breaks through the wave 1 (or wave A) extreme. In other words, enter the trade in halves as shown in Figure 7.22. The Fibonacci section above provides details on calculating targets.

There is a reason that wave 2 is usually sharp. The completion of wave 1 signals (to an Elliott wave practitioner, at least) that the larger trend has reversed. If, after months of trending lower, a five wave rally is evident on the 60-minute EURUSD chart, then the correct move is to wait for the wave 2 correction to play out in order to get bullish. In more traditional parlance:

FIGURE 7.22 1–2 Base with Entries
Source: Chart created on TradeStation®, the flagship product of TradeStation Technologies, Inc.

buy the dip. As the expected wave 2 correction unfolds, the majority of market participants assume that the downtrend is back under way. In actuality, the decline is just a correction within a new bull market (whether a wave 2 or wave B). If, as often happens, the wave 2 (or wave B) correction is sharp, then a greater percentage of market participants return as bears. These traders enter short positions, expecting a break of the low (the origin of wave 1 or wave A). The psychology that is present in a sharp wave 2 correction leads to the wave 3 (or wave C) explosion to the upside. Without a deep wave 2 (or wave B) correction to convince most market participants that the trend is still down, a strong wave 3 (or wave C) advance cannot happen. Those that went short must cover their short positions, which exacerbates the bullish move. This is why the third leg of a move, whether wave 3 of a five wave impulse or wave C of a three wave correction, is often the strongest.

The Ending Diagonal Reversal

Although the 1–2 Base setup often presents the most profitable opportunities, trading the ending diagonal reversal is probably my favorite setup. The move following an ending diagonal is just as fast as a third wave, and it tends to happen instantly; which provides instant gratification. More patience is required when attempting to catch a third wave because price often traces out a series of first and second waves (Figure 7.23) before the third wave explodes.

An ending diagonal is referred to as a *wedge* by traditional chartists. Ending diagonals are fairly common. In fact, you should expect an ending diagonal in the fifth wave position if the third wave was exceptionally strong. As the diagonal unfolds, draw a line connecting the tops of waves 1 and 3 (if the diagonal is down, then connect the bottoms of waves 1 and 3). Also, draw a line connecting the bottoms of waves 2 and 4 (if the diagonal is up, then connect the tops of waves 2 and 4). Wave 5 of the diagonal usually ends near the line that is extended from waves 1 and 3. Occasionally, wave 5 will exceed this line before reversing. Elliott called this a "throwover."

Again, I enter in halves. Enter the first half of the position where the line that is extended from waves 1 and 3 intersects with price. Enter the second half of the position on a break of the line that is extended from waves 2 and 4. Ending diagonals are usually fully retraced, so the profit target is the origin of the diagonal. See Figure 7.24.

Catching a Wave 4 Terminus

If you take profits following a third wave and want to rejoin the trend or if you simply wish to add to your position on a pullback, then an optimal

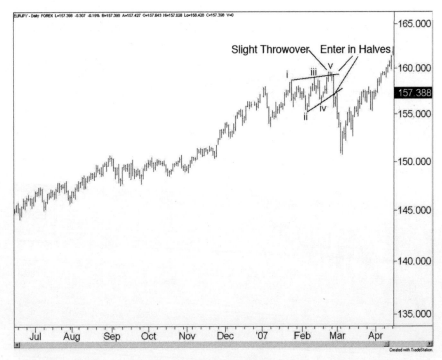

EURJPY - Daily FOREX L=157.398 -0.307 -0.19% B=157.398 A=157.427 O=157.643 H=157.828 Lo=158.428 C=157.398 V=0

FIGURE 7.23 A Series of First and Second Waves
Source: Chart created on TradeStation®, the flagship product of TradeStation Technologies, Inc.

time to do so is upon completion of a wave 4 correction. Remember, fourth waves are often more shallow than second waves. If wave 2 is a zigzag, then wave 4 will most likely unfold as either a flat or a triangle (the tendency for two corrective waves in a five wave impulse to be different in character, one deep and one shallow, is known as *alternation*). Again, the most important aspect is form, but Fibonacci relationships among waves of the same degree help with timing. Wave 4 will most commonly retrace roughly 38.2 percent of wave 3 (Figure 7.25). A stop is placed below the top of wave 1 since waves 4 and 1 cannot overlap (be careful if you trade very short term on intraday charts as intraday price spikes can result in overlapping of waves 1 and 4).

Wave C of a Flat Correction

Wave C of a flat correction (or any correction, for that matter) is always an impulse. If the final leg of a correction is not an impulse, then

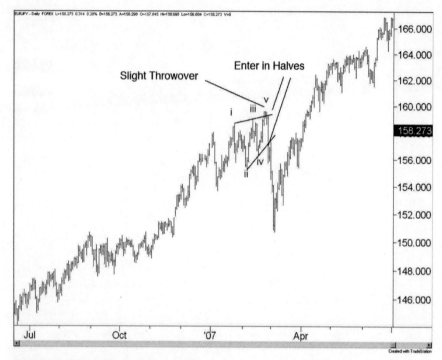

FIGURE 7.24 Ending Diagonal Trade Setup
Source: Chart created on TradeStation®, the flagship product of TradeStation Technologies, Inc.

the correction that has unfolded is not a simple flat or zigzag, but rather a complex correction that is composed of a string of simple corrections. Trading wave C of a zigzag is explained earlier in the 1–2 Base section.

After a five wave impulse, always expect a correction. If, after the three wave correction, price has failed to retrace even 38.2 percent of the previous five wave impulse, then probability is high that a larger flat correction is unfolding and that the initial three wave correction was just wave A of the larger A–B–C correction. Remember, in a flat, the wave B retracement is usually deep. In an expanded flat, wave B actually exceeds the origin of wave A. Expanded flats are common in FX, perhaps because the high degree of leverage leads to extreme price spikes that temporarily exceed the origin of wave A. This tendency makes trading wave C of a flat frustrating sometimes. Still, the reward-to-risk ratio in such instances warrants taking action. As mentioned, flats tend to occur as fourth waves. However, triangles also occur as fourth waves. When attempting to trade the end of the

FIGURE 7.25 Wave 4 into Wave 5
Source: Chart created on TradeStation®, the flagship product of TradeStation Technologies, Inc.

correction (wave C), you do not know whether the pattern will resolve as a flat or a triangle. For this reason, it is important to keep risk tight when trading wave C of a flat. The example in Figure 7.26 of the EURJPY shows that wave B retraced nearly 100 percent of wave A before wave C began.

SOME DIFFERENCES BETWEEN STOCKS AND FX IN ELLIOTT

The path of the stock market represents human progress and regress, construction and destruction, growth and decay. The stock market is always in one of the five waves at the largest degree of trend. *Degrees of trend* are not covered in this book in detail, but an introduction is in order. As described in *Elliott Wave Principle*, "All waves may be categorized by relative size, or degree. The degree of a wave is determined by its size and position

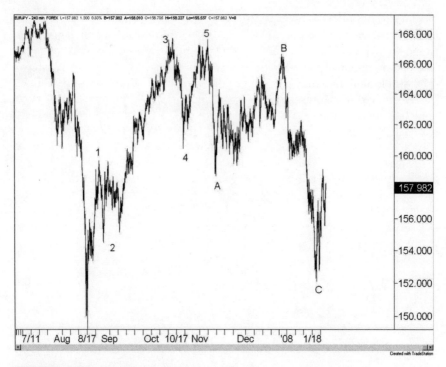

FIGURE 7.26 A Wave C Selloff

Source: Chart created on TradeStation®, the flagship product of TradeStation Technologies, Inc.

relative to component, adjacent, and encompassing waves." Elliott named nine degrees of waves. From largest to smallest, they are:

- Grand Supercycle
- Supercycle
- Cycle
- Primary
- Intermediate
- Minor
- Minute
- Minuette
- Subminuette

The authors go on to say, "Cycle waves subdivide into Primary waves that subdivide into Intermediate waves that in turn subdivide into Minor waves, and so on."[12]

Additionally, "the theory of the spiraling Wave Principle suggests that there exist waves of larger degree. . .Perhaps Homo sapiens himself is one stage in the development of hominids, which in turn are one stage in the development of even larger waves in the progress of life on Earth."[13] The stock market is the best barometer that we have to measure human progress, and it is interesting to look at it within the perspective of very long term waves. For example, the creation of the U.S. stock market in 1792 with the Buttonwood Agreement may have been the beginning of wave 5 of Grand Supercycle degree. Wave 5 of Grand Supercycle degree divides into five waves of Supercycle degree, and so on. As mentioned, the stock market is always in one of the five waves at the largest degree of trend, which then subdivides into smaller degrees of trend. Waves in currencies are not as intuitive though.

Currencies have only been freely traded since the early 1970s, so the largest degree visible on charts is Cycle. There is a much more important distinction between counting long-term waves in the stock market and currencies. The theory of the spiraling wave principle (see Figure 7.27) in

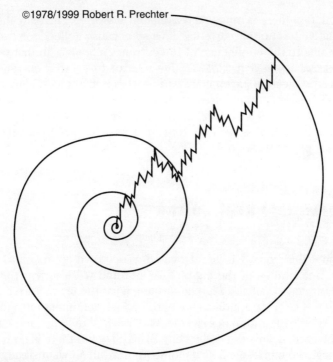

©1978/1999 Robert R. Prechter

FIGURE 7.27 Spiraling Wave
Source: Courtesy of Elliott Wave International, Inc.

stocks means that the trend is always up at the largest degree of trend. Of course, history tells us that humans do undergo enormous setbacks from time to time (these would be the corrections in waves 2 and 4), but the setbacks are still reactionary in nature and eventually give way to progress. Examples include the South Sea bubble in the 1720s and the Great Depression in the 1930s (and maybe the great asset bubble that is coming to an end right now in 2007).

So, while the stock market is a barometer of human progress in the long term, what do currencies represent in the long term? First of all, what is currency? Many people mistake currency for money, or something that is backed by something tangible. If you approached the U.S. Treasury and asked to exchange your dollars for something tangible, you would get nothing. As Prechter notes in *Conquer the Crash*, "The dollar is 'backed' primarily by government bonds, which are promises to pay dollars. So today, the dollar is a promise backed by a promise to pay an identical promise. If the Treasury will not give you anything tangible for your dollar, then the dollar is a promise to pay nothing."[14] If currency is not really anything in the first place, then determining what currency movements represent is quite difficult.

I think that there is only one reasonable answer. A currency that gains value relative to another currency does so because collective psychology as it pertains to the confidence of the currency's holders in that currency improves. A currency that loses value relative to another currency does so because collective psychology as it pertains to the confidence of the currency's holders in that currency deteriorates. How do we measure collective psychology as it pertains to the confidence of a currency's holders? The only way to do it is with the tools that measure sentiment. The wave principle is one of these tools.

BUILDING UP FROM LOWER TIME FRAMES

Throughout this book, I have advocated a top-down approach to market analysis. Get an idea of the big picture first and work down from there. With Elliott wave analysis, I am confirming what the big picture indicates. For example, COT data indicates a euro bearish sentiment extreme and a U.S. dollar bullish sentiment extreme. The trader should be on the lookout to buy the euro against the dollar (buy EURUSD), but there is no reason to blindly begin buying, especially if momentum is still down. Instead, wait for a sizeable rally. If the rally happens, then examine the hourly chart. If the rally occurred in five waves, then buy the ensuing correction (this is the 1–2 Base). Much more patience is required than if you had blindly bought but the probability of a successful outcome is greater and risk is clearly defined (the origin of the rally). In this way, you are working from the bottom up with the wave principle in order to confirm what the top down (big picture) is telling you.

The fractal nature of markets makes this a logical approach. Remember, the patterns that occur at smaller degrees of trend will bond together to form the patterns at larger degrees of trend. Once you see five waves in one direction on an hourly chart, then probability is high that at least one more five wave move will occur (in the case of an A–B–C correction) and possibly two more five wave moves (in the case of a 1–2–3–4–5 impulse).

MULTIYEAR FORECAST FOR THE U.S. DOLLAR

Of course, it is still tempting to examine long-term charts in an attempt to forecast what will happen over the next several years. There are always a number of potential outcomes; therefore, there is always more than one valid wave count. The goal of the Elliottician is to find the highest probability count. There are certain guidelines, or characteristics of waves, that make one count more probable than another. Study the resources listed in the Notes in order to familiarize yourself with the guidelines.

Regarding the U.S. dollar, the peak in 1985 appears to have formed after an impulse that sported an extended fifth wave. Did the U.S. dollar complete a fifth wave of very large degree near 165 in 1985? If that is the case, then the decline from the July 2001 high is wave C. Wave A was from 164.72 to 85.42, which was a 48.14 percent decline. Wave B was a complex correction (3–3–3) and ended at 121.00. A potential terminus for wave C then is where wave C is equal to wave A in percentage terms, which is at 62.75. That level would potentially provide support for a multiyear bottom to form. This remains the favored outlook as long as the USD Index is below the 2005 high of 92.63. Today, the USD Index is near 75.00, so long-term risk is shifting higher with every tick lower. The favored count is outlined in Figure 7.28.

MULTIYEAR FORECAST FOR THE USDJPY

The USDJPY is probably the clearest chart in terms of long-term wave formation in FX. It is probable that a five wave decline is unfolding from the 1971 high. Wave 3 of the decline is extended and divides perfectly into five

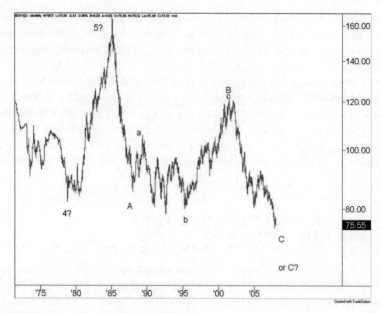

FIGURE 7.28 USD Dollar Index Monthly Bars
Source: Chart created on TradeStation®, the flagship product of TradeStation Technologies, Inc.

FIGURE 7.29 USDJPY Monthly Bars
Source: Chart created on TradeStation®, the flagship product of TradeStation Technologies, Inc.

waves itself. Wave 4 completed in late July 2007 in the form of a triangle (a–b–c–d–e). Expectations then are for a drop below the 1995 low at 81.12 to complete wave 5. Since triangles lead to terminal thrusts, the fifth wave low will give way to a rally that could reach the triangle extreme near 150.00. In summary, expect price to come under 81.12 before a multidecade low is registered. The long-term USDJPY count is detailed in Figure 7.29.

CONCLUSION

Knowledge of the wave principle will allow you to time your trades to the day and sometimes even to the hour. This chapter should serve as a brief introduction to the wave principle. It is strongly recommended that you study the resources listed in the Notes. Always remember though, nothing is a sure thing, and risk must always be defined and at the forefront of consideration before taking any trade.

CHAPTER 8

Putting It All Together

Most traders, especially in FX, lose money. Speculation in any instrument is difficult because it is an unnatural activity for the human brain. Emotional impulses, hope, greed, and fear mean that market tops will occur when traders are extremely long, and market bottoms will occur when traders are extremely short. Imagine a boat. When too many people are on one side of the boat, it tips over. Similarly, the market tops when too many traders are long and bottoms when too many traders are short. A market does not reward the majority of its participants.

Many, if not most, participants forget the dynamic that I have described and allow themselves to become overly excited and join the crowd when the better decision is to distance themselves from the crowd. I am not advocating that you be a contrarian for the sake of simply being a contrarian. You will never make any money that way, either. There is a time when the best decision is to sit with your position (do nothing) and ride the trend. As soon as signs of a sentiment extreme appear (such as magazine covers, strong language in headlines or predictions within headlines, a wave count indicating that the currency pair is completing five waves in one direction, or extreme COT readings), exit and reassess the situation.

WHY MOST TRADERS LOSE

There is the plain fool, who does the wrong thing at all times everywhere, but there is the Wall Street fool, who thinks he must trade all

*the time. No man can always have adequate reasons for buying and
selling...*

—Edwin Lefévre, *Reminiscences of a Stock Operator*
(John Wiley & Sons, Inc., 1923, p. 31)

This quote from *Reminiscences of a Stock Operator* warns of one of
the mistakes most responsible for a lot of lost money: over-trading. The
only time to trade is when the odds are in your favor.

A simple way to solve an over-trading problem is to take a longer-term
approach. Begin by trading end of day prices. Once you feel confident and
disciplined enough, move to intraday charts but always determine your
bias from a daily chart or higher. Determining a bias from a daily chart
and confirming it with the wave pattern from the intraday charts works
well for me.

DEVELOPING A PROCESS

There is a lot of information in this book, so how do you combine it into ac-
tionable ideas? I wrote in the first chapter that the goal of this book was to
"present a framework that you can use to gauge where the market of your
choice is in the never ending oscillation between optimism and pessimism;
and then trade accordingly." The methods in this book should help you do
just that. Once you have gauged the psychological state of the market, then
the odds are in your favor. For example, suppose the EURUSD has been
rallying for the past few weeks. Should you go with the trend or fade it?
Develop a process that works for you using the methods in this book that
would answer a similar question.

For example, scan the financial news headlines by searching for the
specific currency at Google news. If the language is strong or takes a directional stand, then watch for a reversal. If the language is mundane, then the
trend is likely to continue. A mundane headline would be something along
the lines of "Euro rallies against Dollar." Be sure to check major financial
news magazine covers as well. Always be aware of current COT positioning. If the COT indicators are near 0 or 100, then look to trade the reversal.
If the COT indicators are not yet extreme, then the trend will likely continue. What does the picture look like from an Elliott wave perspective?
If you see a clear Elliott wave pattern, then you will have a good idea as
to what the highest probability move is. Combine the various sentiment
measures. If the sentiment measures conflict with one another, then look
for an opportunity elsewhere. When the measures confirm one another,
exploit the opportunity.

IN CONCLUSION

At the end of the day, sentiment is what matters. Go back to Chapter 3 and look at the charts at the end of that chapter with the COT indicators. Every single top and bottom on the charts is accompanied by a reading of 0 or 100; regardless of "news" or "fundamentals." A reversal occurs, and there is inevitably a reason put forth for the reversal. You will know though that there is only one real reason (sentiment extreme), and better yet, that reason (the sentiment extreme) can be anticipated and acted on profitably.

Notes

Chapter 1: The Argument for a Sentiment-Based Approach

1. Bernard Baruch, foreword to *Extraordinary Popular Delusions and the Madness of Crowds*, by Charles Mackay (Boston: L. C. Page, 1932).
2. Ibid.
3. Robert R. Prechter, Jr., *The Wave Principle of Human Social Behavior* (Gainesville, GA: New Classics Library, 1999), 152.
4. Edwin Lefévre, *Reminiscences of a Stock Operator* (New York: John Wiley & Sons, 1923), 10, 124, 130–131, 177, 180, 234, 286.

Chapter 2: The Problem with Fundamental Analysis

1. E. Lefévre, *Reminiscences of a Stock Operator* (New York: John Wiley & Sons, 1923), 124.
2. R. R. Prechter, Jr., *The Wave Principle of Human Social Behavior* (Gainesville, GA: New Classics Library, 1999), 147.
3. Ibid., 151.
4. Ibid., 152.
5. Ibid., 153.
6. R. Yamarone, *The Trader's Guide to Key Economic Indicators* (Princeton, NJ: Bloomberg Press, 2004), 72–73.
7. Ibid., 11.
8. Ibid., 15.
9. Ibid., 16.

Chapter 3: The Power of Magazine Covers

1. "The Death of Equities: How Inflation Is Destroying the Stock Market," *Business Week* (August 13, 1979): 54.

2. "To Rescue the Dollar," *Time* (November 13, 1978): 18.

3. Ibid.

4. "Petropanic and the Pound," *The Economist* (February 2, 1985): 12.

5. S. Hochberg and P. Kendall, March 2000 Elliott Wave Financial Forecast.

6. "Euroshambles," *The Economist* (September 16, 2000): 23.

7. Ibid.

8. "Europe's Economies—Stumbling Yet Again?," *The Economist* (September 16, 2000): 77.

9. "Let the Dollar Drop," *The Economist* (February 7, 2004): 65.

10. Ibid.

11. "The Disappearing Dollar," *The Economist* (December 4, 2004): 9.

12. "The Sadness of Japan," *The Economist* (February 16, 2002): 11.

13. "An Economy Singed," *The Economist* (June 22, 2002): 13.

14. Ibid.

15. "Calling for the Band to Strike Up," *The Economist* (June 22, 2002): 67.

16. T. Arnold, J. Earl, and D. North, "Are Cover Stories Effective Contrarian Indicators?," *Financial Analysts Journal, 63*(2), (2007): 70–75.

17. R. Prechter, 1999. *The Wave Principle of Human Social Behavior* (Gainesville, GA: New Classics Library, 1999), 334.

Chapter 4: Using News Headlines to Generate Signals

1. G. Noble, "The Best Trading Indicator—The Media," *Stocks & Commodities* (1989).

Chapter 5: Sentiment Indicators

1. N. Taleb, *The Black Swan: The Impact of the Highly Improbable* (New York: Random House, 2007); L. Williams, *Trade Stocks & Commodities with the Insiders: Secrets of the COT Report* (Hoboken, NJ: John Wiley & Sons, 2005).

2. E. Lefévre, *Reminiscences of a Stock Operator* (New York: John Wiley & Sons, 1923), 68.

Chapter 6: The Power of Technical Indicators

1. M. Fisher, *The Logical Trader* (Hoboken, NJ: John Wiley & Sons, 2002).

2. J. W. Wilder, Jr., *New Concepts in Technical Trading Systems* (Edmonton, AB, Canada: Trend Research, 1978).

Chapter 7: Explanation of Elliott Wave and Fibonacci

1. R. Prechter and A. Frost, *Elliott Wave Principle: Key to Market Behavior* (Gainesville, GA: New Classics Library, 1978), 31.

2. http://www.elliottwave.com/info/.

3. B. Mandelbrot, *The Fractal Geometry of Nature* (New York: W.H. Freeman, 1983).

4. R. Prechter and A. Frost, *Elliott Wave Principle: Key to Market Behavior* (Gainesville, GA: New Classics Library, 1978), 19.

5. Ibid., 31.

6. Ibid., 37.

7. Ibid., 102–103.

8. Ibid., 103.

9. Ibid., 108.

10. Ibid., 109.

11. Ibid., 80.

12. Ibid., 26.

13. Ibid., 167.

14. R. Prechter, *Conquer the Crash: You Can Survive and Prosper in a Deflationary Depression* (Hoboken, NJ: John Wiley & Sons, 2002), 98.

Index

191